William Shakespeare

Measure for Measure

Edited by

Grace Ioppolo

Commentary by

Leon Rubin

The Applause Shakespeare Library
Measure for Measure

Edited by Grace Ioppolo
Commentary by Leon Rubin
General Series Editor: John Russell Brown
Copyright © 2001 Applause Books

All rights reserved. No part of this publication may be reproduced or transmitted in any form, by any means, electronic or mechanical including photocopying, recording, or any information storage or retrieval system now known or to be invented, without permission in writing from the publishers, except by a reviewer who wishes to quote brief passages in connection with a review written for inclusion in a magazine, newspaper or broadcast.

Library of Congress Cataloging-in-Publication Data

Library of Congress Card Number: 00-111095

British Library Cataloging-in-Publication Data
A catalog record for this book is available from the British Library.

ISBN: 1-55783-387-7

APPLAUSE THEATRE BOOKS
151 W46th Street, 8th Floor
New York, NY 10036
Phone: (212) 575-9265
FAX: (646) 562-5852
email: info@applausepub.com

COMBINED BOOK SERVICES LTD.
Units I/K, Paddock Wood Distribution Centre
Paddock Wood, Tonbridge, Kent TN 12 6UU
Phone: (44) 01892 837171
Fax: (44) 01892 837272

SALES & DISTRIBUTION, HAL LEONARD CORP.
7777 West Bluemound Road, P.O. Box 13819
Milwaukee, WI 53213
Phone: (414) 774-3630
Fax: (414) 774-3259
email: halinfo@halleonard.com
internet: www.halleonard.com

Table of Contents

General Preface to the Applause Shakespeare Library

This edition is designed to help readers see and hear the plays in action. It gives an impression of how actors can bring life to the text and shows how certain speeches, movements, or silences take on huge importance once the words have left the page and become part of a performance. It is a theatrical edition, like no other available at this time.

Everyone knows that Shakespeare wrote for performance and not for solitary readers or students in classrooms. Yet the great problem of how to publish the plays so that readers can understand their theatrical life is only beginning to be tackled. Various solutions have been tried. The easiest—and it is an uneasy compromise—is to commission some director or leading actor to write a preface about the play in performance and print that at the beginning of the volume, followed by a critical and historical introduction, the text and notes about verbal difficulties, a textual introduction, and a collation of variant reading as in any other edition. Another easy answer is to supply extensive stage directions to sort out how characters enter or exit and describe any gestures or actions that the text explicitly requires. Both methods give the reader little or no help in realizing the play in performance, moment by moment, as the text is read.

A more thorough-going method is to include some notes about staging and acting among the annotations of meaning, topical references, classical allusions, textual problems, and so forth. The snag here is that the theatrical details make no consecutive sense and cannot deal with the larger issues of the build-up of conflict or atmosphere, the developing impression of character, or the effect of group and individual movement on stage. Such notes offer, at best, intermittent assistance.

In the more expensive one-volume editions, with larger-than-usual formats, yet another method is used to include a stage history of the play showing how other ages have staged the play and describing a few recent productions that have been more than usually successful with the critics. The snag here is that unavailable historical knowledge is required to interpret records of earlier performances. Moreover, the journalistic accounts of productions which are quoted in these histories are liable to emphasize what is unusual in a production rather than the opportunities offered to actors in any production of the play, the text's enduring theatrical vitality. In any case, all this material is kept separate from the rest of the book and not easily consulted during a reading of the text.

The Applause Shakespeare goes further than any of these. It does the usual tasks expected of a responsible, modern edition, but adds a very special feature: a continuous commentary on the text by a professional director or a leading actor that considers the stage life of the play as its action unfolds. It shows what is demanded from the actors—line by line where necessary—and points out what decisions about interpretation have to be made and the consequences of one choice over another. It indicates where emotional climaxes are placed—and where conflicting thoughts in the character's mind create subtextual pressures beneath the words. Visual statements are noted: the effect of groups of figures on stages, of an isolated figure, or of a pair of linked figures in a changing relationship; the effect of delayed or unexpected entries, sudden departures, slow or processional exuents, or a momentarily empty stage. Everything that happens on stage comes within the notice of this commentary. A reader can "feel" what the play would be like in action.

What the commentary does not do is equally important from the reader's point of view. It does not try to provide a single theatrical reading of the text. Rather if offers a range of possibilities, a number of suggestions as to what an actor might do. Performances cannot be confined to a single, unalterable realization: rather, each production is continually discovering new potential in a text, and it is this power of revelation and revaluation that the commentary of the Applause Shakespeare seeks to open up to individual readers. With this text in hand, the play can be produced in the theatre of the mind, creating a performance suitable to the moment and responsive to individual imaginations. As stimulus for such recreations, the commentary sometimes describes the choices that particular actors or directors made in famous productions, showing what effect words or physical performances have achieved. The purpose here is to supplement what a reader might supply from his or her own experience and imagination, and also to suggest ways in which further research might discover more about the text's theatrical life.

   The commentary is printed in a wide column on the page facing the text itself, so that reference can be quickly made at any particular point or, alternatively, so that the commentary can be read as its own narrative of the pay in action. Also, to the right of the text are explanations of difficult words, puns, multiple meanings, topical allusions, references to other texts, etc. All of these things will be found in other editions, but here it is readily accessible without the eye having to seek out the foot of the page or notes bunched together at the rear of the volume. The text is modernized in spelling. Both stage directions and punctuation are kept to a minimum—enough to make reading easy, but not so elaborate that readers are prevented from giving life to the text in whatever way they choose. As an aid to reading aloud, speech-prefixes are printed in full and extra space used to set speeches apart from each other; when the text is read silently, each new voice can register clearly. At the rear of the book, an extended note explains the authority for the text and a collation gives details of variant readings and emendations.

   In many ways the Applause Shakespeare is a pioneering edition, responding to an old challenge in a new way and trying to break down barriers to understanding that have proved very obstinate for a long time. Further volumes are in preparation and editorial procedures are being kept under review. Reports on the usefulness of the edition, and especially of its theatrical commentary, would be most welcome. Please write to John Russell Brown, c/o Applause Books, 151 West 46th Street, 8th Floor, New York, NY 10036.

INTRODUCTION

Many critics have labeled *Measure for Measure* a "problem play" or a "dark comedy" and have criticized Shakespeare for using the play to problematize or darken the genre of comedy. Other critics have applied these labels to the play's thematic content, rather than its dramatic form, and have criticized Shakespeare for using the play to problematize and darken his perception of human nature. Because both of these views fault Shakespeare, either for producing a flawed artistic genre or a flawed artistic vision, the play has been seriously misunderstood and misinterpreted. Shakespeare deliberately designed *Measure for Measure* to challenge, perplex, and disturb us. In both its form and content, the play forces us to confront our deepest inhibitions and to reveal and accept our most hidden and repressed feelings and emotions. When a member of the theatrical or reading audience leaves the play feeling disturbed or uncertain, Shakespeare has not failed but succeeded brilliantly.

By genre a comedy, the play is unlike any of Shakespeare's comedies written before it, such as *Midsummer Night's Dream*, *Much Ado About Nothing*, or *Twelfth Night*, all of which celebrate the reconciling power of romantic love. Yet, *Measure for Measure* marks the first of Shakespeare's comedies written during the Jacobean age, that is, the years of 1603-1625 dominated by the rule of King James I ("Jacobus" in Latin), and it introduces a darker comic vision than we are accustomed to seeing before 1603. Shakespeare's earlier comedies, written in the Elizabethan age under the rule of Elizabeth I (1556-1603), are often termed "festive" because of their amusing portrayals of the courtship of young couples who wittily struggle to establish equal, loving relationships that will allow them ultimately to endow their social world with peace, stability, and happiness.

However, *Measure for Measure* strays from this usual Shakespearian pattern by uncomfortably portraying the anti-courtship of young couples (including the implied courtship of the prostitute Kate Keepdown and her immoral lover, the liar Lucio). These couples painfully struggle to re-establish less hurtful relationships that may not offer happiness, much less peace or stability, to a corrupted social world. Rather than implying that love can redeem the social order from corruption, as Shakespeare's "festive" comedy usually does, his Jacobean comedy demonstrates that love cannot totally regenerate or be regenerated by a social world that can never free itself of its inherent corruption. Although a "comedy" is defined by the *Oxford English Dictionary* as "a stage-play of a light and amusing character, with a happy conclusion to its plot" or as "that branch of the drama which adopts a humorous or familiar style, and depicts laughable characters and incidents," this comedy fails in both definitions, as the play is neither light nor happy in its conclusion nor comfortably humorous or laughable. In fact, the basic nature of comedy is missing from *Measure for Measure*: the only comic moments come in the subplot of the pimps, bawds, and their customers who see fornication and not love or marriage as the foundation for all social interaction. What this comic play teaches us which its Shakespearian predecessors do not is that comedy is much closer to tragedy than we are willing to accept, a conclusion Shakespeare seems to have reached by 1604, the midpoint of his writing career. The play, by nature, is not "problematic" or "dark" but is instead a reflection of the problematic and dark nature of human behavior.

We know from court records that the King's Men, Shakespeare's acting company, performed *Measure for Measure* for King James at least once at the royal palace of Whitehall on December 26, 1604 as part of St. Stephen's Night celebrations. Judging from the play's allusions to political events in 1604, Shakespeare probably composed it shortly before this performance. Many critics have suggested that the Duke's complaints in I.i,

> I love the people,
> But do not like to stage me to their eyes.
> Though it do well, I do not relish well
> Their loud applause and aves vehement,

echo those of James I, already known in the first years of his reign to be reclusive and uncomfortable with public spectacle and crowds. In addition, the Duke's decision to adopt the disguise of a Friar in order to heal his subjects seems to reflect James' belief that he was destined to join a religious order rather than serve as King of England, Scotland, and Wales. The reign of James shifted moral and social concerns as much as political concerns; for example, the strong female figure of Elizabeth, whose reign attempted to secure more rights for women, was replaced by James, who reinforced male values and once again relegated women to subservient roles. Elizabethan matriarchy was displaced by Jacobean patriarchy. Thus, critics theorize that the play "flatters" James with its portrayal of a powerful male ruler who secretly, but nearly omnisciently and omnipotently, uses religion to solve the many moral and social problems of his subjects. Recent feminist critics also emphasize the play's insistence on patriarchy and the silencing of female voices. Yet these theories misinterpret the play as much as those which dismiss the play as "problematic" or "dark," for Shakespeare makes clear throughout the play that the Duke is as troubled as those he attempts to punish or to heal, and the patriarchy he imposes fails to contain men *and* women within a restrictive social order and hierarchy. Such an unflattering portrayal was not a simple attempt to flatter the monarch. The play clearly works on much deeper and more complex levels.

More certain sources for the play than the character of James I appear in Giraldi Cinthio's 1565 prose romance, *Hecatommithi* and George Whetstone's 1578 play, *Promos and Cassandra*. Both texts adapted the folktale of a woman who attempts to gain mercy for her imprisoned brother (or, in some versions, her imprisoned husband) from a corrupt magistrate. After the woman submits to the magistrate's demand that she sleep with him to secure her brother's release, she is told that her brother has been executed. She then demands justice from the country's ruler, who sentences the magistrate to marry the woman, in order to restore her honor, and then to be executed. The woman pleads for mercy for her new husband, and his life is spared. Shakespeare also adapted this story by introducing the character of Mariana to take the sister's place in bed with the magistrate, thereby allowing the sister to remain a virgin suitable for marriage with the ruler, who conspires in the story's outcome. Although the "bed-trick" substitution was a common theatrical convention in Elizabethan and Jacobean drama, other playwrights used it to give male characters the power to rape and thereby punish unwilling or assertive female characters. In this play, and in his next comedy *All's Well That Ends Well*, Shakespeare uniquely uses the bed-trick to endow female characters with the power to reintegrate sexuality and marriage and thereby redeem their unwilling male partners. However, Shakespeare also acknowledges that Angelo can refuse to accept the restorative power of Mariana's gift of her body.

Shakespeare did more in *Measure for Measure* than simply rework a folktale or dramatic convention. Having recently finished *Hamlet* and *Troilus and Cressida*, he appeared determined to continue these plays' examinations of how repressed sexual desire serves as the basis of human thought, action, behavior, and most importantly, conflict. Although previous critics have cited religious mercy, forgiveness, and repentance as the dominant themes of *Measure for Measure*, the play first and foremost focuses on the legal and illegal, moral and immoral, and regenerative and destructive uses of sexuality. While Shakespeare's preceding comedies examine the status of romantic relationships before sexual consummation, this play examines the status of such relationships after sexual consummation. In the early plays, marriage brings social sanction to sexuality, but in this later play, marriage seems incapable of reconciling couples or their society and sexuality cannot be socially or morally sanctioned. Claudio and Juliet have entered into a "clandestine" marriage, a privately-made contract, recognized in this age as a legal marriage although it lacked the civil or religious ceremony (Mariana also believes that her former contract with Angelo has already produced a legal marriage). Indeed, marriage remains a clandestine and conspiratorial institution in this play, as the bed-trick emphasizes. Isabella's first response in I.iii to the news of Claudio's arrest for impregnating Juliet is, "Oh, let him marry her," but this obvious solution is dismissed as no longer relevant. This dismissal of the reconciliatory power of marriage ironically foreshadows others, for in V.i Shakespeare will dismiss Isabella's (and Mariana's) power to accept or reject the man who hastily offers her marriage. Throughout the play, then, marriage serves as an insignificant and imbalanced mode of union in a play whose very title demands equal measure and balance in all things.

Rather than promising the emotional joy and physical bliss outlined by Oberon at the end of *A Midsummer Night's Dream*, for example, sexual union in *Measure for Measure* brings discord, denunciation, and the threat of death. The private world of sexuality becomes publicized and legislated, and those, such as Pompey, Mistress Overdone, and Lucio, who operate in the previously underground world of the illegal, but flourishing, sex trade, serve as this society's most celebrated representatives of the inability to repress sexuality. Although this world can be venereally diseased (as Lucio and his friends acknowledge in I.ii), Shakespeare also demonstrates that it can be healthy and regenerative, as evidenced by the birth of Claudio and Juliet's baby by the end of the play. The practice of sexuality between two willing partners is not the problem in the play; how that practice of sexuality is interpreted by others is the problem. Pompey's question to Escalus in II.i, "Does your worship mean to geld and splay all the youth of the city?"

and Escalus's response, "No," prompt Pompey's warning, "In my poor opinion they will to't then." Pompey and, particularly, Lucio, whose name suggests "light" or "illumination," are the most articulate about the true, sexual nature of all the citizens of Vienna.

Measure for Measure exposes hypocrites. Many critics have faulted Isabella as the play's most dangerous hypocrite and cite her "selfishness" or "egotism" in her pronouncement, "More than our brother is our chastity" and her refusal to sleep with Angelo to save Claudio's life. Termed "frigid" or "repressed," Isabella has, until the recent rise of feminist studies, been criticized for being merciless to her brother when she herself demands mercy for him from Angelo. Yet, Shakespeare makes it more than clear that Isabella has acted morally and shrewdly in refusing to surrender her virtue to Angelo, for he intends to execute Claudio regardless of whether she accepts his sexual proposition. Even when Angelo believes he has slept with her, not yet knowing that Mariana took her place, he refuses to order a countermand to save Claudio, much to the moral disgust of the Duke, who must resort to subterfuge to stop the execution. Isabella's function in the play is to serve as comparison to the play's more dangerous hypocrites, Angelo and the Duke. Angelo, to his credit, at least recognizes his hypocrisy in demanding non-consensual fornication with Isabella when he has condemned her brother for consensual fornication. For Angelo, the man who "scarce confesses / That his blood flows," fornication and lechery are synonymous; he does not see sexual intercourse, as Claudio does, as "most mutual entertainment" and insists that it must not be mutual when he attempts to force it on Isabella. Although penitent at the play's end, we as audience have no great faith that he deserves the love and undying devotion of Mariana, to whom he does not offer marriage but to whom he is forcibly married. If we are disturbed that Shakespeare denies Isabella the voice to answer the Duke's offer of marriage, we are made even more uncomfortable with Mariana's voiced offer that she craves "no better man" than Angelo. Yet both Isabella and Mariana demonstrate in their seeming acceptances of the Duke and Angelo that they cannot be measured as "better" or "worse" than their male partners.

Like Isabella and Angelo, the Duke is a self-admitted virgin who does not believe that "the dribbling dart of love / Can pierce a complete bosom" and later asserts that he was not "much detected for women, he was not inclined that way." Shakespeare seems uncomfortable with self-cloistered people, including these three characters, whose moral arrogance closes them off from others as well as themselves. But the Duke is more troublesome a hypocrite; as a ruler and as a man, he fails to admit how his continuing hypocrisy continually recreates this immoral world. He does acknowledge his "fault" in having given his people too much moral scope, but he refuses to use his "tyranny" to gall them into the moral boundaries required by social convention, boundaries that he himself oversteps. He abdicates his role as moral and political ruler of his people to test Angelo, whom he already suspects of moral hypocrisy, and usurps the role of the Friar to serve as a seeming spiritual leader. As Lucio ironically puts it, "it was a mad, fantastical trick of him to steal from the state and usurp the beggary he was never born to." Although the Duke angrily objects when Lucio describes him as a fornicator and pander, the Duke indeed serves as a broker in sexuality when he convinces Mariana to substitute for Isabella in Angelo's bed. The Duke had earlier rebuked Juliet that her willingness to sleep with Claudio before marriage meant that her "sin" was "of heavier kind than his," yet he tells Mariana when he convinces her to sleep with Angelo, "To bring you together, 'tis no sin." Thus, his moralistic lecture to Pompey for being "a bawd, a wicked bawd," whose life "is so stinkingly depending" could, ironically, be addressed to himself, a fact he apparently realizes.

Lucio, termed the play's "fantastic" and most public liar and hypocrite, is the play's most honest spokesman, for he understands the difference between the commercial nature of fornication, as practiced by Mistress Overdone and her prostitutes, and loving, mutual sexuality, as practiced by his friends Claudio and Juliet. He recognizes and praises Isabella's virginity, but later teaches her how to use it to manipulate Angelo. Only Lucio understands the deeply ironic element required to judge human nature and action because he knows that others' interpretation of an action can often be more dangerous than the action itself. For this reason he serves not simply as a lewd, comic villain but as a mirror in which the Duke can see himself. Lucio speaks the ironic and literal truth in calling "the Duke of dark corners" an "unweighing fellow" for the Duke must resort to measure for measure because he has failed to weigh his own actions equally. Lucio's moral pronouncement at his entrance in I.ii that "grace is grace, despite of all controversy," that mercy is mercy in spite of all debate, proves the play's most wise and spiritually beneficent statement.

Although we can recognize by the end of the play the repentance of Isabella, who pleads for mercy for the life of the man who she thinks has killed her brother, and the repentance, however credible, of Angelo, the Duke's spiritual growth remains ambiguous. He seems to have no qualms about torturing Isabella until the last lines of the play into believing that her brother is dead so that he can resurrect him and thereby test her moral worthiness as his potential wife. He also willingly plays a hypocrite throughout the first part of V.i in publicly rebuking both Isabella, whom he has instructed to lie about having slept with Angelo, and Mariana, whom he has seemingly prostituted, and then in threatening both women with imprisonment. But the Duke is neither a complete villain nor a complete hero. He, like Isabella, Angelo, and the others, represents the complexities of correctly judging complexly-layered characters. Neither he nor we as audience can view enough of his multi-dimensional character to contain it or define it with certainty. Thus the Duke may appear deceitful at the same time he appears honest, for Shakespeare demands that his audience re-evaluate themselves when they attempt to evaluate him and the other characters.

Above all, this brilliantly constructed and crafted play demands that the audience recognize that human nature cannot be judged through one extreme or the other and must not be judged only in comparison with others in weighing "measure for measure." Instead of relative moral values that rise or fall in comparison or measure with others, society can only function with a fixed set of moral values that nonetheless values and judges compassionately. The Duke, Angelo, and Isabella all learn that each must adhere to the same, unchanging moral code and that each person must measure himself against himself not against others. The inhabitants of Vienna's world learn that "truth is truth / To th'end of all reck'ning." Like grace, truth is truth, despite all controversy.

Due to its complex themes and characters, the play uses a similarly complex style and structure. Readers of the play, particularly actors, find the language, difficult to follow and sometimes nonsensical, as in this passage in the Duke's opening speech:

> Of government, the properties to unfold
> Would seem in me t'affect speech and discourse,
> Since I am put to know that your own science
> Exceeds in that the lists of all advice
> My strength can give you.

In essence, some dialogue in the play seems needlessly convoluted, with twisted syntax which separates subject from verb and thus prevents the listener from understanding both the agent of action (the subject) and the action (the verb) in the sentences. This unusual syntax, usually due to the repeated use of relative and dependent clauses, may interfere with the actors' and audience's ability to convey and understand both the theatrical dialogue and action. Some critics have suggested that such linguistic style is not typically "Shakespearian," and they argue that the play must have been cut or revised by another author, possibly Thomas Middleton, after Shakespeare retired from the theatre. Their basic argument is that Shakespeare was much too skilled a playwright to have deliberately written such difficult dramatic language.

Yet, Shakespeare's linguistic style changed and evolved throughout his career, and his later Jacobean plays also use linguistically difficult styles. By the midpoint of his career, Shakespeare seemed willing to experiment with both unusual themes and styles, mirroring content with form. The Duke's opening speech needs to appear difficult to follow in order to emphasize from the outset of the play that the Duke feels distracted and uncomfortable in his role of a too lenient ruler. Some of his speeches seem disconnected and unclear because Shakespeare wants to portray him as ill at ease. The complexly structured and highly persuasive arguments of Isabella and the shrewd responses of Angelo in II.ii and II.iv demonstrate that Shakespeare was superbly capable of using dialogue to define and enhance his characters. Also, the bawdy and terse comments of Lucio and Pompey throughout the play also show that Shakespeare could use a linguistically spare style. In the later scenes of the play, beginning in Act III, Shakespeare begins to rely on prose, rather than verse, to reflect the common world in which the Duke and his subjects are now immersed. In essence, Shakespeare suited the linguistic style to the character, plot, and setting. There is no external or internal evidence, such as the play's stylistic complexities, to support the argument that this play was co-written or revised by another author.

Similarly, the play's structure seems to violate Shakespeare's typical use of the classic model of the five act structure, which demands a dramatic climax at the end of the third act with a subsequent denouement. Some critics believe that the second confrontation between Angelo and Isabella in II.iv constitutes the play's climax. These critics are also disturbed by the fact that all of Act III and almost all of Act IV after the first scene are set in a prison, and by the apparent decision by Shakespeare or his acting company to perform Acts III and V as single scenes rather than as a series of scenes, as in Acts I and II. Thus, the structure of the play from III.i until the conclusion seems to be faulty, especially since it seems to be built on too many coincidental or suddenly introduced events and characters (such as Barnardine and Ragozine) for which the audience has not been prepared in the earlier Acts. The Duke's reemergence in Act II.iii after his disappearance in Act I should not seem sudden or unexpected; he has made it clear in I.iii that he will be watching Angelo and the rest of his subjects from the shadows. We are reminded of him throughout the scenes in Acts I and II in which he is absent by other characters' constant references to him. The Duke's soliloquy which concludes Act III serves as the play's climax because it forces him into morally dangerous action from which there is no turning back, the release of Isabella from Angelo's demand and the substitution of Mariana in her "contracting" with Angelo. The prison settings for Acts III and IV remind us that the Duke must suffer the physical imprisonment of those he rules. The seamlessness of Acts III and V as single scenes heighten the tension and intensify the singleness of the actions, all of which are controlled by the Duke.

Shakespeare's audience may have been as disturbed by the play as many modern audiences have been, for there are no records of the play being performed between late December 1604 and 1623, when the play was first printed. However, theater records of the age are very scanty, so the play may have enjoyed further performances, at least in Shakespeare's lifetime, both in public theatres, such as the Globe, and in private houses, such as Whitehall Palace. Many of Shakespeare's most popular plays were printed within a few years of the first performance in cheap quarto editions, but we have no extant quarto of this play, suggesting that the play was not a popular success after its early performances. Although some scholars speculate that Middleton or another of Shakespeare's contemporaries adapted the play before 1623 (see Textual History), the earliest surviving adaptation of the play is William Davenant's *The Law Against Lovers*, performed in 1662. Charles Gildon also adapted the play as *Measure for Measure, or Beauty the Best Advocate* in 1700.

Extant records document that Shakespeare's version of the play was performed in 1660 (after the reopening of the public theatres which had been closed by the Puritans in 1642) and many times in the 18th century, with such prominent actors as Sarah Siddons playing Isabella and John Kemble playing the Duke. The play was performed less frequently in the 19th century, although the first recorded American performance took place in New York's Park Theatre in 1818. The play has been performed throughout the 20th century, with its most controversial and innovative productions staged since 1945, especially in the treatment of three of the play's most difficult issues, the ambiguous character of the Duke, his unexpected proposal to Isabella, and her lack of dialogue to offer a response. Peter Brook's 1950 production at the Shakespeare Memorial Theatre in Stratford-on-Avon, England, was praised for its strong emphasis on character, particularly in centering the play on Angelo, played by John Gielgud, rather than on the Duke. The Royal Shakespeare Company's 1970 production, also in Stratford, shocked audiences with Isabella's silent dismissal of the Duke's proposal. Later productions in the 1970's, including Jonathan Miller's 1973 production at the National Theatre in London, presented Isabella not only refusing to take the Duke's hand after his proposal but scornfully and contemptuously stalking offstage in response. The 1979 BBC Shakespeare Series videotape production presented the play more traditionally, with a Duke who insisted on remaining central to the play, an attractive and virtuous Isabella who accepted him, and a repentant Angelo. Theater productions in the 1980's and 1990's have continued this trend, especially in the 1983 Royal Shakespeare Company production in which the Duke, played by Daniel Massey, clearly realizes that he has fallen in love with Isabella, played by Juliet Stevenson, at his first meeting with her. He treats her with loving tenderness in their subsequent scenes, temporarily giving into his emotions by embracing and kissing her in IV.iii when she cries at his news of Claudio's execution, releasing her only at the entrance of Lucio who has observed the embrace. Massey's engaging and multi-faceted performance, including his developing love for Isabella, demonstrates that the dramatic inconsistencies and weaknesses in the written text about which so many critics have complained can disappear in performance. *Measure for Measure*, so seemingly fixed in its message but so fluid in its interpretations, can continue to excite and move theatre audiences as it has for four hundred years.

Grace Ioppolo
University of Reading, England

INTRODUCTION TO COMMENTARY

This commentary deals with the challenge for a director and actors who wish to stage the mysterious and complex play. I have tried to stay close to the text, attempting to travel back through time to understand what Shakespeare himself was imagining when he wrote the play. However, it is a play that also adapts well to the modern stage and modern technology and the director and actors of our time have few problems understanding the characters and themes of *Measure for Measure*. There are a number of key questions concerning character interpretation that are open to various solutions. Isabella can be seen as a pure, strong and brave woman of conviction, or a cold intellectual out of touch with emotions and feelings and terrified of her own hidden passions. The Duke can be played as a semi-comic, indecisive man who is frequently out of his depths, or a wise ruler who is determined to test those around him as he himself ventures on a journey of understanding. Lucio might be played as a witty parasite, devoid of care about anything expect his own comfort and survival, or as a man who really does have a keen understanding of the true nature of those around him. The play allows these polarities and also more complex interpretations that combine them within the characters, subtly balanced one way more than the other. Measure for Measure is also a play that adapts easily to modern dress and diverse settings. The central themes concerning justice, mercy, corruption, hypocrisy, purity, power and sexual attraction are found within any culture, society or time period. This is a play that excites and delights directors with these themes and rich array of characters, and having finished the commentary as a professional theatre director specialising in Shakespeare, I too am now anxious to stage it somewhere in the world. I thank John Russell Brown for his wise and good-humoured advice and my colleague, Dr. Signy Henderson for her scrupulous attention to detail. My thanks also to Middlesex University, England for the continual and generous support for my theatre department.

Leon Rubin
Middlesex University, England
July 1997

Measure
For
Measure

CHARACTERS

THE DUKE OF VIENNA, named
   Vincentio

ISABELLA, a novice° and sister to
   Claudio

ANGELO, the Duke's deputy

ESCALUS, an elderly lord

THE PROVOST

CLAUDIO, a young gentleman

LUCIO, a fantastic°

ELBOW, a simple constable

FROTH, a foolish gentleman

POMPEY, a clown

JULIET, betrothed to Claudio

MARIANA, a young gentlewoman
   once betrothed to Angelo

FRIAR THOMAS

FRIAR PETER

A JUSTICE

VARRIUS

ABHORSON, an executioner

BARNARDINE, a dissolute prisoner

MISTRESS OVERDONE, a bawd

FRANCISCA, a nun

BOY, a servant to Mariana

LORDS, GENTLEMEN, OFFICERS, CITIZENS and SERVANTS

ACT I

Scene i   *Enter* DUKE, ESCALUS, [*and* LORDS.]

DUKE   Escalus.

ESCALUS   My lord.

DUKE   Of government, the properties to unfold
   Would seem in me t'affect° speech and discourse,

a candidate for nun

person fantastical in action or
dress

1-15   The text of *Measure for Measure* is always
drawn from the First Folio, as it is the only authorita-
tive version. Unlike many other play texts in the First
Folio, this one has few scenic indications and only
economical references to stage directions. This first
scene is typical, in that there is no specific reference
to the time or place. It could be exterior, outside the
palace, or in a small chamber or indeed in a more
public state-room. Later in the scene and again in the
second we get the first references to the location of
the play in Vienna (1.i.44 and 1.ii.87). Although there

to pretend to like

Since I am put to know that your own science   5
Exceeds in that the lists of all advice
My strength can give you. Then no more remains
But that to your sufficiency as your worth is able,
And let them work. The nature of our people,
Our city's institutions, and the terms   10
For common justice, you're as pregnant° in
As art and practice hath enrichèd any
That we remember.   [*He gives* Escalus *a paper.*]
                    There is our commission,°
From which we would not have you warp.°
                              [*To a* Lord.] Call hither,
I say, bid come before us Angelo.   [*Exit* Lord.]   15
What figure° of us, think you, he will bear?
For you must know, we have with special soul
Elected him our absence to supply,
Lent him our terror,° dressed him with our love,
And given his deputation° all the organs   20
Of our own power. What think you of it?

Escalus   If any in Vienna be of worth
          To undergo such ample grace and honor,
          It is Lord Angelo.

                         Enter Angelo.

Duke   Look where he comes.

Angelo   Always obedient to your grace's will   25
         I come to know your pleasure.

Duke   Angelo,
         There is a kind of character in thy life
         That to th'observer doth thy history
         Fully unfold. Thyself and thy belongings
         Are not thine own so proper as to waste   30
         Thyself upon thy virtues,° they on thee.
         Heaven doth with us as we with torches do,
         Not light them for themselves, for if our virtues
         Did not go forth of us, 'twere all alike
         As if we had them not. Spirits are not finely touched   35
         But to fine issues, nor nature never lends

are various further references to Vienna and other associated mid-European places, events and people, the King of Hungary for example, the names of the characters suggest a more mixed and wider allusion to a number of societies. Shakespeare is using Vienna as a vehicle for a plot that sits as well in England or in Italy of the period. Most productions in the last thirty years or so have set the play in modern settings ranging from Mussolini's Italy to Freud's Vienna and modern day Sienna.

knowledgeable

We can assume at least some attendants are present and at least one must exit to find Angelo. The presence of Lords, as suggested in the stage direction, is not referred to at any point in the dialogue and can be ignored in production if the scene is to be played intimately rather than grandly and publicly. Similarly the entrance of the Duke can be ceremonial or simple and private.

written command

deviate

representation

After a short speech, in which the Duke praises Escalus and his skills in government, he quickly gets down to business as Angelo is summoned. As there is no expression of surprise by Escalus, we can assume that the Duke has announced his imminent departure before the start of the scene. The Duke abruptly hands a document to Escalus (13) and issues a warning not to contradict any of the commands therein. The speed at which this first scene moves is emphasized by the command to seek Angelo, "Call hither", sitting on the end of the same-verse line that ends his brief introductory address to Escalus (14).

power to invoke fear

appointment as deputy

16-23 Escalus must feel put on the spot as the Duke looks him hard in the eye and suddenly asks his opinion of Angelo. He is also probably feeling surprised or upset that he himself has not been chosen as deputy. He is forced to give a positive response regardless of his real opinion.

24-48 Angelo enters only moments after being summoned, suggesting perhaps that he has been expectantly waiting close at hand. Again the swiftness of the rhythm and the Duke's excitement in the scene are emphasised in the verse structure in the shared verse lines (24 and 26). In the latter example, the Duke cannot contain himself long enough for Angelo to finish his ritual greeting. Angelo may feel baffled by the first half of the Duke's speech that sings Angelo's praises without explanation. Suddenly, however, there is a change of rhythm and style as the Duke gets back to business with "Hold therefore, Angelo" (42). This short, unfinished line probably indicates an intake of breath and a brief pause

alluding to the parable of the talents (Matthew 25:14-30)

The smallest scruple of her excellence
But, like a thrifty goddess, she determines
Herself the glory of a creditor,
Both thanks and use. But I do bend my speech   40
To one that can my part in him advertise;
Hold therefore, Angelo.
In our remove, be thou at full ourself.
Mortality and mercy in Vienna
Live in thy tongue and heart. Old Escalus,   45
Though first in question,° is thy secondary.°
Take thy commission.

ANGELO   Now, good my lord,
Let there be some more test made of my mettle
Before so noble and so great a figure
Be stamped upon it.

DUKE   No more evasion.   50
We have with a leavened° and preparèd choice
Proceeded to you, therefore take your honors.
                    [*He gives* ANGELO *a paper.*]
Our haste from hence is of so quick condition
That it prefers itself and leaves unquestioned
Matters of needful value. We shall write to you   55
As time and our concernings shall importune,
How it goes with us, and do look to know
What doth befall you here. So fare you well.
To th' hopeful execution do I leave you
Of your commissions.

ANGELO   Yet give leave, my lord   60
That we may bring you something on the way.

DUKE   My haste may not admit it,
Nor need you, on mine honor, have to do
With any scruple. Your scope° is as mine own,
So to enforce or qualify the laws   65
As to your soul seems good. Give me your hand,
I'll privily° away. I love the people,
But do not like to stage me to their eyes.
Though it do well, I do not relish well
Their loud applause and aves° vehement,   70

before the Duke explains his decision to leave Angelo in full command. An inadvertent reaction by the watching, silent Escalus may explain the specific reference to "Old Escalus" (45).

seniority   subordinate

tempered

52-75   The Duke is already beginning his exit. He may have stage business to complete, picking up suitcases or putting on a hat or coat, as he repeatedly talks about the need for haste in his departure. He never stops to explain why he is leaving and his reluctance to discuss matters further may be part of this avoidance of explanation.

range of power

secretly

welcomes

Nor do I think the man of safe discretion
That does affect it. Once more, fare you well.

ANGELO   The heavens give safety to your purposes.

ESCALUS   Lead forth and bring you back in happiness.

DUKE   I thank you, fare you well.   *Exit.*   75

ESCALUS   I shall desire you, sir, to give me leave
To have free speech with you, and it concerns me
To look into the bottom of my place.
A power I have, but of what strength and nature
I am not yet instructed.   80

ANGELO   'Tis so with me. Let us withdraw together,
And we may soon our satisfaction have
Touching that point.

ESCALUS   I'll wait upon your honor.   *Exeunt.*

Scene ii   *Enter* LUCIO *and two other* GENTLEMEN.

LUCIO   If the Duke, with the other Dukes, come not to
composition° with the King of Hungary, why then all
the Dukes fall upon the King.

FIRST GENTLEMAN   Heaven grant us its peace, but not the King of
Hungary's.   5

SECOND GENTLEMAN   Amen.

LUCIO   Thou conclud'st like the sanctimonious pirate that went
to sea with the ten Commandments but scraped one out of
the table.

SECOND GENTLEMAN   Thou shalt not steal?   10

LUCIO   Aye, that he razed.°

FIRST GENTLEMAN   Why, 'twas a commandment to command the captain and all the rest from their functions: they put forth to

75-83   The short silence, indicated by the half-line at the Duke's exit, "I thank you, fare you well" (75), suggests the stunned responses of Angelo and Escalus to the whirlwind scene that has just turned both their lives upside down. Escalus breaks the silence with an expression of his uncertainty, confusion and possible distress. Angelo may be feeling pleased but gives little away with his response.

The scene ends with a firm reminder that it is Angelo now who holds all power as Escalus accepts and acknowledges the situation with his final "I'll wait upon your honor". The final reaction of Angelo as the scene ends is important as he can either looked happy and confident at the thought of his new power or, as in some productions, a civil servant out of his depths reluctantly taking up his new duties.

Scene ii

1-15   Lucio and the two gentlemen enter already in the middle of a discussion about local politics. The scene is probably set in the streets of Vienna, as various characters come and go. The constant entrances and exits throughout the scene suggest a bustling and noisy environment where all classes of people pass by each other regularly; in the background there is probably a series of additional street life. The earthy low-life atmosphere needs to contrast to the Court of the first scene. This is an opportunity in some productions to establish the red light aspects of the play as the dominant tone, as for example in director Nicholas Hytner's 1987 production at the Royal Shakespeare Company in Stratford described by critic Nicholas de Jongh as "a teeming metropolitan meeting point, loud with police sirens, thronged by punkish youths...", (*The Guardian*, 12 October, 1988).

The verse of the first scene has been replaced by blunt prose as the three men stop to chat about the Duke, thereby linking this scene to the previous one. The political references quickly give way to general joking, appropriate to the low-life street setting.

agreement

scraped out

steal. There's not a soldier of us all that in the thanksgiving
before meat° do relish the petition well that prays for peace.   15

SECOND GENTLEMAN   I never heard any soldier dislike it.

LUCIO   I believe thee, for I think thou never wast where grace
was said.

SECOND GENTLEMAN   No? A dozen times at least.

FIRST GENTLEMAN   What? In meter?   20

LUCIO   In any proportion or in any language.

FIRST GENTLEMAN   I think, or in any religion.

LUCIO   Aye, why not? Grace is grace, despite° of all
controversy,° as for example: thou thyself art a wicked
villain, despite of all grace.   25

FIRST GENTLEMAN   Well! There went but a pair of shears° between
us.

LUCIO   I grant, as there may between the lists° and the velvet.
Thou art the list.

FIRST GENTLEMAN   And thou the velvet. Thou art good velvet,   30
thou'rt a three piled-piece,° I warrant thee. I had as lief° be
a list of an English kersey° as be piled° as thou art piled for
a French velvet.° Do I speak feelingly now?

LUCIO   I think thou dost, and indeed with most painful feeling
of thy speech. I will, out of thine own confession, learn to   35
begin° thy health, but whilst I live, forget to drink after
thee.

FIRST GENTLEMAN   I think I have done myself wrong, have
I not?

SECOND GENTLEMAN   Yes, that thou hast, whether thou art   40
tainted° or free.

Enter MISTRESS OVERDONE.

LUCIO   Behold, behold, where Madam Mitigation° comes. I have
purchased as many diseases under her roof as come to—

grace before meals

15-40   The tone of the humor sinks lower as the three of them tease each other about venereal disease. There is probably physical horseplay as they pun about the velvet on the clothes they may be wearing and the velvet used to cover venereal sores. This sexual repartee is a preliminary to the entrance of Mistress Overdone (41).

in spite
debate

scissors

cheap fabric edgings

i.e., bald from venereal disease
  gladly
coarse cloth   bald
French: i.e., venereally diseased
velvet: wearer of velvet

begin a toast to

infected

41-54   As Mistress Overdone enters the stage in the distance the three see her and are thereby encouraged in their humorous exchanges about sexual diseases. She is not spoken to for a further fifteen lines, probably indicating the length of time it takes her to reach them. As with a similar entrance of the Nurse in *Romeo and Juliet* (II.iv.89), this probably suggests a comic stage-picture as she arrives. Perhaps her costume is extravagant and garish and

sexual relief

SECOND GENTLEMAN   To what, I pray?

LUCIO   Judge.   45

SECOND GENTLEMAN   To three thousand dolors° a year.

FIRST GENTLEMAN   Aye and more.

LUCIO   A French crown° more.

FIRST GENTLEMAN   Thou art always figuring° diseases in me, but
    thou art full of error, I am sound.   50

LUCIO   Nay, not, as one would say, healthy, but so sound as
    things that are hollow. Thy bones are hollow, impiety° has
    made a feast of thee.

FIRST GENTLEMAN   [*To* MISTRESS OVERDONE.] How now, which of
    your hips has the most profound sciatica°?   55

MISTRESS OVERDONE   Well, well. There's one yonder arrested and
    carried to prison was worth five thousand of you all.

SECOND GENTLEMAN   Who's that, I pray thee?

MISTRESS OVERDONE   Marry,° sir, that's Claudio, Signior Claudio.

FIRST GENTLEMAN   Claudio to prison? 'Tis not so.   60

MISTRESS OVERDONE   Nay, but I know 'tis so. I saw him arrested,
    saw him carried away, and which is more, within these
    three days his head to be chopped off.

LUCIO   But after all this fooling, I would not have it so. Art
    thou sure of this?   65

MISTRESS OVERDONE   I am too sure of it, and it is for getting
    Madam Julietta with child.

LUCIO   Believe me, this may be. He promised to meet me two
    hours since, and he was ever precise in promise-keeping.

SECOND GENTLEMAN   Besides, you know, it draws something near   70
    to the speech we had to such a purpose.

FIRST GENTLEMAN   But most of all agreeing with the proclamation.

LUCIO   Away, let's go learn the truth of it.
                                [*Exeunt* LUCIO *and two* GENTLEMEN.]

sorrows, pun on *"dollars,"* for-
eign coins

she may walk with a limp, suggested by the first gentleman's reference to "sciatica", although, as in
Jonathan Miller's production, she has also been
interpreted as "a coldly, professional madame concerned only with her week's takings" (*Times*, 24
November 1973).

coin, with pun on "baldness"
  caused by venereal disease
representing

The references to her brothel make her
profession clear to the audience.

wickedness

nerve disease

by Mary, an exclamation

54-73   It is not clear from the context why she has
arrived at this moment but the immediacy of her discussion of Lucio's situation suggests that she has
arrived hastily to tell everyone about her distress. Her
first two exchanges with the gentlemen betray an
aggressive tone as she firstly retorts, when teased
about sciatica, that Lucio is "worth five thousand" of
them and secondly snaps back "but I know 'tis so"
(61) when contradicted rhetorically by the first gentleman about the fate of Claudio. She is clearly agitated by the situation with Claudio and her own lack
of customers. Her news abruptly changes the rhythm
of the scene as Lucio and the others hurry off to find
out what has happened with Claudio (73).

MISTRESS OVERDONE   Thus, what with the war, what with the
    sweat,° what with the gallows, and what with poverty, I am   75
    custom-shrunk.°

Enter POMPEY.

How now? what's the news with you?

POMPEY   Yonder man is carried to prison.

MISTRESS OVERDONE   Well, what has he done°?

POMPEY   A woman.   80

MISTRESS OVERDONE   But what's his offense?

POMPEY   Groping for trouts in a peculiar river.°

MISTRESS OVERDONE   What? Is there a maid° with child by him?

POMPEY   No, but there's a woman with maid° by him. You have
    not heard of the proclamation, have you?   85

MISTRESS OVERDONE   What proclamation, man?

POMPEY   All houses° in the suburbs of Vienna must be plucked
    down.

MISTRESS OVERDONE   And what shall become of those in the city?

POMPEY   They shall stand for seed.° They had gone down too   90
    but that a wise burger° put° in for them.

MISTRESS OVERDONE   But shall our houses of resort in the suburbs
    be pulled down?

POMPEY   To the ground, mistress.

MISTRESS OVERDONE   Why here's a change indeed in the   95
    commonwealth! What shall become of me?

POMPEY   Come, fear not, you, good counselors lack no clients.
    Though you change your place,° you need not change your
    trade. I'll be your tapster° still. Courage! There will be pity
    taken on you. You that have worn your eyes almost out in   100
    the service,° you will be considered.   [*A noise within.*]

MISTRESS OVERDONE   What's to do here, Thomas Tapster? Let's

sweating-sickness

customer shrunk

74-76   For a moment Mistress Overdone is left alone in the foreground and is allowed a brief direct address to the audience as she bemoans her state. It is also possible to play this sequence additionally to an on-stage audience of bystanders in the street, as in the Caribbean set production by director Michael Rudman that featured a "plump, eyerolling Mistress Overdone" who loved to play to her street audience (*Now*,14 April 1981).

The speedy rhythm of the scene continues as Pompey enters, interrupting her brief chat with the audience.

unintentional pun on "forni-
cated with"

78-105   Pompey is presumably referring to Claudio during this next exchange, as he describes the arrest. Editors have often been worried about the contradiction of events, but in reality events are moving too fast for an audience to be concerned about such details. The dialogue is funny and fast, full of sexual jokes and innuendo as Pompey explains the impact of the new draconian laws to an increasingly distressed Mistress Overdone. She exits rapidly as the officers, Provost and others enter on the way to the prison.

i.e., seducing forbidden
women

unmarried woman, uninten-
tional pun on "virgin"

female child

brothels

lie fallow

businessman   bought

location

ale-drawer, i.e., her pimp

i.e., prostitution

withdraw.

POMPEY   Here comes Signior Claudio led by the Provost to
prison, and there's Madam Juliet.   105

Exeunt POMPEY *and* MISTRESS OVERDONE.

Enter PROVOST, CLAUDIO, JULIET, OFFICERS, LUCIO,
and two GENTLEMEN.

CLAUDIO   Fellow, why dost thou show me thus to th' world?
Bear me to prison where I am committed.

PROVOST   I do it not in evil disposition,
But from Lord Angelo by special charge.

CLAUDIO   Thus can the demi-god, authority,   110
Make us pay down for our offense by weight
The words of heaven, on whom it will, it will;
On whom it will not, so, yet still 'tis just.

LUCIO   Why how now, Claudio? Whence comes this restraint?

CLAUDIO   From too much liberty, my Lucio, liberty.   115
As surfeit is the father of much fast,
So every scope by the immoderate use
Turns to restraint. Our natures do pursue,
Like rats that ravin° down their proper bane,°
A thirsty evil, and when we drink, we die.   120

LUCIO   If I could speak so wisely under an arrest, I would send
for certain of my creditors. And yet, to say the truth, I had
as lief° have the foppery° of freedom as the mortality of
imprisonment. What's thy offence, Claudio?

CLAUDIO   What but to speak of would offend again.   125

LUCIO   What, is't murder?

CLAUDIO   No.

LUCIO   Lechery?

CLAUDIO   Call it so.

PROVOST   Away, sir, you must go.   130

CLAUDIO   [*To the* PROVOST.] One word, good friend. Lucio, a

devour   a poison

106-113 The entrance of this group should be formally organised and designed for maximum effect; it is not a casual entrance but part of a formalized, public displaying of the prisoner. A crowd of townspeople is also useful to make the point that part of the punishment for Claudio is in the way he is being displayed to that crowd. The audience in the theatre also becomes part of that town audience as the Provost shows Claudio to the world. The elevated verse that Claudio breaks into is in contrast to the ignominious situation he finds himself in; he is as upset by this public humiliation as he is by the larger situation itself. However, in contrast, after this parade the Provost seems to deliberately step aside with the officers and allow Claudio time to ask Lucio for assistance; perhaps in this way he demonstrates some sympathy for Claudio even at this early point in the play. He probably moves away and does not listen to the conversation, thus allowing privacy. Due to this distance Claudio must call out to him that he is ready to go when his conversation with Lucio is over.

gladly   folly

word with you.

Lucio   A hundred if they'll do you any good. Is lechery so
    looked° after?

Claudio   Thus stands it with me. Upon a true contract   135
    I got possession of Julietta's bed.
    You know the lady, she is fast° my wife,
    Save that we do the denunciation° lack
    Of outward order.° This we came not to,
    Only for propagation° of a dower°   140
    Remaining in the coffer° of her friends,
    From whom we thought it meet to hide our love
    Till time had made them for us. But it chances
    The stealth of our most mutual entertainment
    With character too gross is writ° on Juliet.   145

Lucio   With child, perhaps?

Claudio   Unhappily, even so.
    And the new deputy, now for the Duke—
    Whether it be the fault and glimpse of newness,
    Or whether that the body public be
    A horse whereon the governor doth ride,   150
    Who newly in the seat, that it may know
    He can command, lets it straight feel the spur;
    Whether the tyranny be in his place,
    Or in his eminence that fills it up,
    I stagger in—but this new governor   155
    Awakes me all the enrollèd° penalties
    Which have, like unscoured° armor, hung by th'wall
    So long that nineteen zodiacs° have gone round,
    And none of them been worn; and for a name°
    Now puts the drowsy and neglected act   160
    Freshly on me. 'Tis surely for a name.

Lucio   I warrant it is. And thy head stands so tickle° on thy
    shoulders that a milkmaid, if she be in love, may sigh it off.
    Send after the Duke and appeal to him.

Claudio   I have done so, but he's not to be found.   165
    I prithee, Lucio, do me this kind service:
    This day, my sister should the cloister enter

watched

firmly tied

proclamation

official ceremony

production   dowry

treasure chest

135-145 After the short exchange with the plain-speaking Lucio (114-134), Claudio is given an opportunity to present his case to the audience and win sympathy. While not denying the fact that he has technically committed an offense, he is able to explain that he was already, by Elizabethan perspectives, as good as married. This is an important moment for the actor as he tries to draw the audience in emotionally to his point of view. Again, the flowery, eloquent verse is in stark contradiction to lowly situation of the moment.

written

146 Lucio's blunt language, "With child", is in humorous contrast to Claudio's poetic description.

146-161 This speech switches completely the tone as Claudio now angrily attacks Angelo and accuses him of abusing his new power.

registered

rusty

years

reputation

precariously

165-183 The scene ends with Claudio appealing to Lucio for help; the tone changes from anger to practical cunning as Claudio explains how his sister can be persuasive with men. Although the scene has in

And there receive her approbation.°
Acquaint her with the danger of my state,°
Implore her, in my voice, that she make friends   170
To the strict deputy. Bid herself assay° him;
I have great hope in that, for in her youth
There is a prone° and speechless° dialect
Such as move° men. Beside, she hath prosperous art
When she will play with reason and discourse,   175
And well she can persuade.

Lucio   I pray she may, as well for the encouragement of the
like,° which else would stand under grievous imposition, as
for the enjoying of thy life, who I would be sorry should be
thus foolishly lost at a game of tick-tack.° I'll to her.   180

Claudio   I thank you, good friend Lucio.

Lucio   Within two hours.

Claudio   Come, Officer, away.   *Exeunt.*

Scene iii   *Enter* Duke *and* Friar Thomas.

Duke   No, holy Father, throw away that thought,
Believe not that the dribbling dart of love
Can pierce a complete bosom. Why I desire thee
To give me secret harbor hath a purpose
More grave and wrinkled than the aims and ends   5
Of burning youth.

Friar Thomas   May your grace speak of it?

Duke   My holy sir, none better knows than you
How I have ever loved the life removed°
And held in idle price to haunt assemblies
Where youth and cost witless bravery keeps.   10
I have delivered to Lord Angelo,
A man of stricture and firm abstinence,
My absolute power and place here in Vienna,

confirmation
condition

try

mercy provoking   word-
    less
persuade

same

i.e., backgammon, with bawdy
    meaning

effect stood still during these important speeches between Claudio and Lucio, the rhythm picks up abruptly on the last three lines, ending with the command from Claudio "Come, Officer, away". The thought that Isabella will speak for him seems to fuel this last, confident cry. All the characters sweep off the stage in a continuation of the procession that we saw at the opening of the scene. Lucio, alone, heads off in a different direction to find Isabella.

<u>Scene iii</u>

1-6   This scene is set somewhere private and interior, away from the earlier public locations; perhaps it is in the friar's cell. In fact, although there are a few open air and public scenes, much of the play takes place in small, enclosed spaces. In production this is often emphasised in order to focus on the secretive, political and claustrophobic elements of the play. In director David Thacker's version, for example, there was "a Vienna of dark corners, uncomfortable prisons and suspended interrogation lights..." (*Financial Times*, 15 May 1985).

cloistered

This scene is extremely brief and best played whilst on the move. It begins with the Duke and Friar Thomas in mid conversation and has a rushed, anxious tone.The emphatic, contrapuntal first word of the Duke, "No", launches the two characters onto the stage, as the Duke refutes the Friar's idea that the intrigue about the Duke's absence concerns a love affair. The very fact that the Friar has thought this is an interesting comment on the character of the Duke.

And he supposes me travelled to Poland,
For so I have strewed it in the common ear,   15
And so it is received. Now, pious sir,
You will demand of me why I do this.

FRIAR THOMAS   Gladly, my lord.

DUKE   We have strict statutes and most biting laws,
The needful bits and curbs to headstrong weeds,   20
Which for this fourteen years we have let slip,
Even like an o'ergrown lion in a cave
That goes not out to prey. Now, as fond fathers
Having bound up the threat'ning twigs of birch,
Only to stick it in their children's sight   25
For terror, not to use—in time the rod
More mocked than feared—so our decrees,
Dead to infliction, to themselves are dead,
And liberty plucks justice by the nose,
The baby beats the nurse, and quite athwart°   30
Goes all decorum.

FRIAR THOMAS   It rested in your Grace
To unloose this tied-up justice when you pleased,
And it in you more dreadful° would have seemed
Than in Lord Angelo.

DUKE   I do fear too dreadful.
Sith° 'twas my fault to give the people scope,   35
'Twould be my tyranny to strike and gall them
For what I bid them do. For we bid this be done
When evil deeds have their permissive pass
And not the punishment. Therefore, indeed, my Father,
I have on Angelo imposed the office,   40
Who may in th'ambush of my name strike home,
And yet my nature never in the fight
To do in slander. And to behold his sway
I will, as 'twere a brother of your order,
Visit both prince and people. Therefore, I prithee,   45
Supply me with the habit, and instruct me
How I may formally in person bear
Like a true friar. More reasons for this action
At our more leisure shall I render you;

19-33 The Duke outlines the reasons for his feigned absence, but the Friar remains unconvinced at the end of this suspiciously brief explanation. The purpose of the scene is to clarify the plot to the audience and to show, through the Friar, a degree of doubt about the motivations for this plot. The Friar actually challenges the Duke vigorously as he jumps in abruptly on the end of the Duke's unfinished verse-line (31).

in the wrong direction

inspiring dread

since

34-54 In response to the Friar's challenge, the Duke varies his explanation and focuses on the plot as a means of testing Angelo, rather than simply a means to restore the authority of the law. The scene ends oddly with a ringing rhyming couplet that leaves the audience hanging in the air as they await the playing out of the story, in relation to the testing of Angelo.

As the Duke exits, after the couplet, the Friar may react in silence, in a way that indicates if he is yet convinced by the Duke's explanations.

Only this one: Lord Angelo is precise,°   50
Stands at a guard with envy, scarce confesses
That his blood flows, or that his appetite
Is more to bread than stone. Hence shall we see,
If power change purpose, what our seemers be.   [*Exeunt.*]

Scene iv   *Enter* ISABELLA *and* FRANCISCA.

ISABELLA   And have you nuns no farther privileges?

FRANCISCA   Are not these large enough?

ISABELLA   Yes, truly; I speak not as desiring more,
But rather wishing a more strict restraint
Upon the sisterhood, the votarists° of Saint Clare.°   5

LUCIO [*Within.*] Hoa? Peace be in this place.

ISABELLA   Who's that which calls?

FRANCISCA   It is a man's voice. Gentle Isabella,
Turn you the key and know his business of him;
You may, I may not, you are yet unsworn.
When you have vowed, you must not speak with men   10
But in the presence of the Prioress,°
Then if you speak, you must not show your face,
Or if you show your face, you must not speak.
                                        [LUCIO *calls within.*]
He calls again. I pray you, answer him.   [*Withdraws.*]

ISABELLA   [*Opening the door.*] Peace and prosperity. Who is't that   15
calls?

                          [*Enter* LUCIO.]

LUCIO   Hail virgin, if you be, as those cheek-roses
Proclaim you are no less. Can you so stead° me
As bring me to the sight of Isabella,
A novice of this place and the fair sister   20

strict

<u>Scene iv</u>

1-6   This scene is set clearly in a convent as Isabella and Francisca enter in mid-conversation. There should be objects or symbols such as candles and crosses to remind us of this throughout the scene. Religious singing might be heard in the background. This repeated device of entrances in mid-flow creates a growing impression of many scenes being played almost simultaneously. In a modern context it would feel as though a camera is panning from scene to scene, focusing in turn on each pair or group as the conversations run on in parallel. The overall-impression created is one of speed and excitement as the plot unravels.

nuns   13th c. Italian saint

The visual impact of Francisca's habit is strong, in contrast, to the colorful costumes in the street scenes earlier. Along with Friar Thomas, Francisca creates the extreme polarity of world view to that of Lucio and the other low-life characters. The extremity of Isabella's attitudes to life is established from the beginning of the scene as she declares that she wishes even "more strict restraint" than is usual, even in such a strict order as St. Clare. Lucio shouts out loudly "Hoa" breaking the genteel, almost silent world of the convent. With this shout he is bringing a last reminder of the outside world into the new world that Isabella is about to choose.

head of the order

7-15   We are reminded in these lines that Isabella has not yet taken vows and that she is still a novice. As a novice, she is not necessarily wearing a habit. If she does wear a habit throughout the play it greatly affects the scenes with Angelo and the final scene when the Duke proposes; in the past, productions have used both options.This speech also reminds Isabella and the audience of the normal world that Isabella will leave behind when she takes vows; never again will she be able to speak normally with a man. Francisca looks hard at Isabella as she says these words as though looking to see if there is any doubt left.

direct

16-46   There is a humorous tension in Lucio's words as he tries but fails to find the right turn of

    To her unhappy brother Claudio?

ISABELLA   Why 'her unhappy brother,' let me ask,
    The rather for I now must make you know
    I am that Isabella and his sister.

LUCIO   Gentle and fair, your brother kindly greets you.   25
    Not to be weary° with you, he's in prison.

ISABELLA   Woe me! For what?

LUCIO   For that which, if myself might be his judge,
    He should receive his punishment in thanks.
    He hath got his friend with child.   30

ISABELLA   Sir, make me not your story.°

LUCIO   'Tis true.
    I would not, though 'tis my familiar sin
    With maids to seem the lapwing° and to jest
    Tongue far from heart, play with all virgins so.
    I hold you as a thing enskied° and sainted,   35
    By your renouncement,° an immortal spirit,
    And to be talked with in sincerity,
    As with a saint.

ISABELLA   You do blaspheme the good in mocking me.

LUCIO   Do not believe it. Fewness° and truth, tis thus: 40
    Your brother and his lover have embraced;
    As those that feed grow full, as blossoming time
    That from the seedness° the bare fallow brings
    To teeming foison,° even so her plenteous womb
    Expresseth his full tilth and husbandry.°   45

ISABELLA   Someone with child by him? My cousin Juliet?

LUCIO   Is she your cousin?

ISABELLA   Adoptedly, as schoolmaids change° their names
    By vain though apt affection.

LUCIO   She it is.

ISABELLA   Oh, let him marry her.

LUCIO   This is the point.   50

phrase to use in this unaccustomed environment. From his clumsy greeting, "Hail virgin, if you be" (16) through to "I hold you as a thing enskied and sainted" (35), Lucio tries hard to select suitable words to use in a convent. However, this is undercut by more earthy phrases such as "his full tilth and husbandry" that slip out. Isabella begins by assuming that Lucio's extravagant verse is designed to mock her, but gradually realizes that he really is trying to communicate a serious message. It is only at line 46 that she understands the first part of his message, "Someone with child by him? My cousin Juliet?"

tedious

dupe

bird that leads others astray

heavenly
worldly renunciation

in a few words

seeding
harvest
plowing and cultivation

exchange

50-72 After his uncertain start to the conversation Lucio now becomes eloquent and passionate as he

The Duke is very strangely gone from hence;
Bore° many gentlemen, myself being one,
In hand and hope of action. But we do learn,
By those that know the very nerves of state,
His giving-out° were of an infinite distance   55
From his true-meant design. Upon his place,
And with full line of his authority,
Governs Lord Angelo, a man whose blood
Is very snow-broth,° one who never feels
The wanton° stings and motions of the sense   60
But doth rebate° and blunt his natural edge
With profits of the mind, study and fast.
He—to give fear to use and liberty,
Which have for long run by the hideous law
As mice by lions—hath picked out an act   65
Under whose heavy sense your brother's life
Falls into forfeit. He arrests him on it,
And follows close the rigor of the statute
To make him an example. All hope is gone,
Unless you have the grace by your fair prayer   70
To soften Angelo. And that's my pith° of business
'Twixt you and your poor brother.

ISABELLA   Doth he so
Seek his life?

LUCIO   Has censured° him already,
And, as I hear, the Provost hath a warrant
For's° execution.

ISABELLA   Alas, what poor   75
Ability's in me to do him good?

LUCIO   Assay the power you have.

ISABELLA   My power? Alas, I doubt.

LUCIO   Our doubts are traitors
And makes us lose the good we oft might win
By fearing to attempt. Go to Lord Angelo,
And let him learn to know, when maidens sue,°   80
Men give like gods, but when they weep and kneel,
All their petitions are as freely theirs

deceived

official announcement

warms to the theme of attacking Angelo. This leads him effortlessly to the plea for her to intercede. Although it comes from such an unreliable source, his description of Angelo as "a man whose blood /Is very snow-broth" (58) is sometimes taken by actors as a useful starting point for understanding Angelo's character.

melted snow
lustful
reduce

essence

70-76   Lucio seems to enjoy his new role as advocate for Claudio and perhaps finds pleasure in the incongruity of his position as a street-wise pimp talking intimately with the novice nun in a convent.

condemned

for his

plead

78-85   Rapidly finishing Isabella's half line by throwing back at her the word "doubt", Lucio presses his point cleverly home and succeeds in persuading Isabella to go and plead for her brother's life.

    As they themselves would owe° them.

ISABELLA   I'll see what I can do.

LUCIO   But speedily!   85

ISABELLA   I will about it strait,
    No longer staying but to give the Mother°
    Notice of my affair. I humbly thank you.
    Commend me to my brother; soon at night
    I'll send him certain word of my success.   90

LUCIO   I take my leave of you.

ISABELLA   Good sir, adieu.   *Exeunt.*

own

prioress

86-91   The rhythm picks up and the scene ends with a rush as Isabella agrees to go immediately, only allowing herself time to announce to the convent her departure. Lucio has deliberately infected Isabella with the urgency of the situation as they both part with a final, hurried shared verse-line.

ACT II

Scene i   *Enter* Angelo, Escalus, Servants, *and a* Justice.

Angelo   We must not make a scarecrow of the law,
          Setting it up to fear the birds of prey,
          And let it keep one shape till custom make it
          Their perch and not their terror.

Escalus   Aye, but yet
          Let us be keen and rather cut a little   5
          Than fall and bruise to death. Alas, this gentleman
          Whom I would save had a most noble father,
          Let but your honor know,
          Whom I believe to be most strait in virtue,
          That in the working of your own affections,   10
          Had time cohered with place, or place with wishing,
          Or that the resolute acting of our blood
          Could have attained th'effect of your own purpose,
          Whether you had not sometime in your life
          Erred in this point, which now you censure him,   15
          And pulled the law upon you.

Angelo   'Tis one thing to be tempted, Escalus,
          Another thing to fall. I not deny
          The jury, passing° on the prisoner's life,
          May in the sworn twelve have a thief or two   20
          Guiltier than him they try. What's open° made to justice,
          That justice seizes. What knows the laws
          That thieves do pass on thieves? 'Tis very pregnant.
          The jewel that we find, we stoop and take't
          Because we see it, but what we do not see,   25
          We tread upon and never think of it.
          You may not so extenuate his offense

ACT II. Scene i

1-16   Angelo, Escalus, servants and a Justice sweep onto the stage, continuing the rapid forward rhythm of the previous scene. Again, the conversation has already begun offstage and is heated as Escalus tries to argue with Angelo. The servants and, possibly, others in the entourage are important to the scene that follows, as Angelo deliberately aims his words publicly, so that everyone will see the steadfastness of his intent.

Angelo uses scathing humour to mock Escalus who has clearly suggested, prior to entering, that Claudio should be treated as a special case. The use of the scarecrow image is designed to mock Escalus and finish the debate. Escalus, however, is determined to press his point and impatiently finishes, or perhaps, interrupts Angelo's verse line "Aye, but yet..." (5). After these first hasty and passionate phrases, Escalus changes tack and challenges Angelo to look into himself and declare that he too has never "erred in this point". As he says this to Angelo, Escalus looks him hard in the eye and for a moment the scene slows down as Angelo pauses before responding after the hanging, unfinished verse-line at the end of Escalus' speech (16). There is tension among the observers on the stage as they await Angelo's reply.

deliberating

openly

17-31   Angelo responds with the simple statement that it is not relevant if he himself is guilty of a similar crime because the law should be applied to crimes when they are discovered; what the law does not know it cannot deal with. He then declares, again very publicly to the onlookers, that he himself should be judged without mercy if he too is ever found guilty of such a crime. These words are given careful emphasis by Angelo and will be remembered by the audience when they, in effect, become the jury towards the end of the play. On the last line of this speech, Angelo loses patience and abruptly breaks

For I have had such faults, but rather tell me
When I, that censure him, do so offend,
Let mine own judgement pattern out my death,   30
And nothing come in partial.° Sir, he must die.

Enter Provost.

ESCALUS   Be it as your wisdom will.

ANGELO   Where is the Provost?

PROVOST   Here, if it like your honor.

ANGELO   See that Claudio
Be executed by nine tomorrow morning.
Bring him his confessor, let him be prepared,   35
For that's the utmost of his pilgrimage.   [*Exit* PROVOST.]

ESCALUS   [*Aside.*] Well, heaven forgive him, and forgive us all.
Some rise by sin, and some by virtue fall.
Some run from brakes° of ice and answer none,
And some condemnèd for a fault alone.   40

Enter ELBOW *and* OFFICERS *with* FROTH *and* POMPEY.

ELBOW   Come, bring them away.° If these be good people in a
commonweal° that do nothing but use° their abuses in
common houses,° I know no law. Bring them away.

ANGELO   How now, sir, what's your name? And what's the matter?

ELBOW   If it please your honor, I am the poor Duke's constable, and 45
my name is Elbow. I do lean upon justice, sir, and do bring in
here before your good honor two notorious benefactors.

ANGELO   Benefactors? Well, what benefactors are they? Are they
not malefactors?

ELBOW   It if please your honor, I know not well what they are, but 50
precise° villains they are, that I am sure of, and void of all pro-
phanation° in the world that good Christians ought to have.

ESCALUS   [*To* ANGELO.] This comes off well, here's a wise° officer.

ANGELO   [*To* ELBOW.] Go to.° What quality are they of? Elbow is

the rhythm of the verse as he declares "Sir, he must die" (31).

prejudiced

31-40 The sharpness and decisiveness of Angelo's words has warned Escalus that the discussion is over and he ceases to argue. The new tone and rhythm of the scene is added to by the rapid entrance of the Provost who receives his curt command to execute Claudio and exits again. There is a stunned silence from the others on the stage as the first real darkness of tone has entered the play. Escalus has a brief aside to the audience, expressing his sorrow at this command, whilst Angelo is dealing with the formalities of the command by signing and handing over, perhaps, an official document.

traps

along

commonwealth   carry out

brothels

41-80 The shadow over the actions of the play is not allowed to linger long, though, as Elbow, Froth, Pompey and various officers explode onto the stage with a lot of noise, commotion and comedy. The scene should be staged to look like a trial, with Escalus as the judge, Elbow as the prosecutor and Pompey as the defending lawyer. At the beginning, it seems as though Angelo will act as judge, but after a few curt lines (44, 49 and 55) he immediately loses patience. He listens in silence a little longer and becomes irritated and leaves with a final, bad-tempered "Hoping you'll find good cause to whip them all" (124).

In contrast, from the beginning of this sequence, Escalus exhibits good humour and is prepared to indulge in a trial in a real sense; he genuinely wants to discover the truth, even if it takes time. In spite of continually confused utterances from the linguistically challenged Elbow, Escalus joins in the mock legal investigation with a series of questions (63, 65 and 67). The main comedy throughout is from Elbow struggling, hopelessly, to choose words that are apposite for a grand court hearing.

exact (used unintentionally), error for "precious"

error for "salavation"

foolish

to the point

your name? Why dost thou not speak, Elbow?   55

POMPEY   He cannot, sir, he's out at elbow.°

ANGELO   What are you, sir?

ELBOW   He, sir, a tapster, sir, parcel° bawd, one that serves a
bad woman, whose house, sir, was, as they say, plucked
down in the suburbs, and now she professes° a hot-house,°   60
which I think is a very ill house too.

ESCALUS   How know you that?

ELBOW   My wife, sir, whom I detest° before heaven and your
honor—

ESCALUS   How? Thy wife?   65

ELBOW   Aye, sir, whom I thank heaven is an honest° woman.

ESCALUS   Dost thou detest her therefore?

ELBOW   I say, sir, I will detest myself also, as well as she,
that this house, if it be not a bawd's house, it is pity of her
life, for it is a naughty house.   70

ESCALUS   How dost thou know that, Constable?

ELBOW   Marry, sir, by my wife, who, if she had been a woman
cardinally° given, might have been accused in fornication,
adultery, and all uncleanliness there.

ESCALUS   By the woman's means?   75

ELBOW   Aye, sir, by Mistress Overdone's means. But as she spit
in his face, so she defied him.

POMPEY   [*To* ESCALUS.] Sir, if it please your honor, this is not
so.

ELBOW   Prove it before these varlets° here, thou honorable° man;   80
prove it.

ESCALUS   [*To* ANGELO.] Do you hear how he misplaces°?

POMPEY   Sir, she came in great with child and longing, saving
your honors' reverence, for stewed prunes.° Sir, we had but
two in the house, which at that very distant time stood, as it   85
were, in a fruit dish, a dish of some three pence—your

i.e., has tattered sleeves

Even as Elbow inadvertently refers to Angelo and Escalus as "varlets", Escalus cannot help delighting in the accidental clowning and tries to include the indifferent Angelo in this unexpected sport: "Do you hear how he misplaces?"

part-time

keeps   bathing house,
    unintentional pun on
    "brothel"

error for "attest"

chaste

error for "carnally"

rascals, error for "honorable
    men"   error for "dis-
    honorable"

mistakes

82-142 Pompey's long-winded account of the events drives Angelo to a rapid exit, but Escalus is prepared to let the hilarious trial continue. As is so often the case in this play, the audience becomes very much the jury, as Pompey sets out the case for the defense. With a dramatic, extravagant gesture, Pompey warms to his role as trial defense lawyer,

brothel fruit, pun on "prosti-
    tutes"

honors have seen such dishes, they are not China-dishes,   but
very good dishes—

ESCALUS   Go to, go to, no matter for the dish, sir.

POMPEY   No indeed, sir, not of a pin,° you are therein in the right.   90
But to the point. As I say, this Mistress Elbow, being, as I say,
with child, and being great-bellied, and longing, as I said,
for prunes, and having but two in the dish, as I said, Master
Froth here, this very man, having eaten the rest, as I said,
and, as I say, paying for them very honestly—for, as you   95
know, Master Froth, I could not give you three pence again.

FROTH   No indeed.

POMPEY   Very well, you being then, if you be remembered,
cracking the stones° of the foresaid prunes.

FROTH   Aye, so I did indeed.   100

POMPEY   Why, very well. I, telling you then, if you be remembered,
that such a one, and such a one, were past cure of the thing
you wot° of, unless they kept very good diet, as I told you.

FROTH   All this is true.

POMPEY   Why, very well then.   105

ESCALUS   Come, you are a tedious fool, to the purpose. What
was done to Elbow's wife that he hath cause to complain of?
Come me to what was done to her.

POMPEY   Sir, your honor cannot come to that yet.

ESCALUS   No, sir, nor I mean it not.   110

POMPEY   Sir, but you shall come to it, by your honor's leave.
And I beseech you, look into Master Froth here, sir, a man
of four-score pound a year, whose father died at Hallowmas.°
Was't not at Hallowmas, Master Froth?

FROTH   All-Hallond Eve.°   115

POMPEY   Why, very well, I hope here be truths. He, sir, sitting,
as I say, in a lower chair, sir, 'twas in the Bunch of Grapes,°
where indeed you have a delight to sit, have you not?

FROTH   I have so, because it is an open room and good for winter.

not worth a pin

and challenges Escalus to look carefully at Froth's innocent face and judge whether he could be guilty of any crime (139-142). The action really does stop for a moment as Escalus indeed looks into the comic, harmless face of the luckless, ineffectual Froth and accepts the point. This is an opportunity for clowning as Elbow has a few seconds to try and look as innocent as he can, no doubt egged on by Pompey.

pits

know

November 1

October 31

i.e., a particular room

POMPEY   Why, very well then, I hope here be truths.   120

ANGELO   This will last out a night in Russia
           When nights are longest there. I'll take my leave
           And leave you to the hearing of the cause,
           Hoping you'll find good cause to whip them all.

ESCALUS   I think no less. Good morrow to your lordship.   125
                                                   Exit ANGELO.
           Now, sir, come on, what was done to Elbow's wife, once more?

POMPEY   Once, sir? There was nothing done° to her once.

ELBOW   I beseech you, sir, ask him what this man did to my wife.

POMPEY   I beseech your honor, ask me.

ESCALUS   Well, sir, what did this gentleman to her?   130

POMPEY   I beseech you, sir, look in this gentleman's face. Good
           Master Froth, look upon his honor, 'tis for a good purpose.
           Doth your honor mark his face?

ESCALUS   Aye, sir, very well.

POMPEY   Nay, I beseech you mark it well.   135

ESCALUS   Well, I do so.

POMPEY   Doth your honor see any harm in his face?

ESCALUS   Why, no.

POMPEY   I'll be supposed° upon a book, his face is the worst
           thing about him. Good then, if his face be the worst thing   140
           about him, how could Master Froth do the Constable's wife
           any harm? I would know that of your honor.

ESCALUS   He's in the right, Constable, what say you to it?

ELBOW   First, an it like you, the house is a respected° house;
           next, this is a respected fellow; and his mistress is a   145
           respected woman.

POMPEY   [*To* ESCALUS.] By this hand, sir, his wife is a more
           respected person than any of us all.

ELBOW   Varlet, thou liest! Thou liest, wicked varlet! The time is yet 149
           to come that she was ever respected with man, woman, or child.

sexually practiced

error for "deposed"

error for "suspected"

144-164 The comedy of the scene builds as Elbow becomes more and more incensed by the situation and his words become increasingly mangled. This all climaxes in an explosion by Elbow as he verbally assaults Pompey with his speech beginning "O thou caitiff! O thou varlet! O thou wicked Hannibal." By this point Escalus himself is delighted with the absurdity of it all and joins in with his own twisted words: "If he took you a box 'oth' ear, you might have your action of slander too." Elbow, completely unaware that he is

POMPEY [*To* ESCALUS.] Sir, she was respected with him before
he married with her.

ESCALUS Which is the wiser here: justice or iniquity? [*To* ELBOW.]
Is this true?

ELBOW [*To* POMPEY.] O thou caitiff°! O thou varlet! O thou   155
wicked Hannibal!° I respected with her before I was married
to her? [*To* ESCALUS.] If ever I was respected with her, or she
with me, let not your worship think me the poor Duke's
officer! [*To* POMPEY.] Prove this, thou wicked Hannibal, or I'll
have mine action of battery° on thee!   160

ESCALUS If he took you a box o'th' ear, you might have your
action of slander too.

ELBOW Marry, I thank your good worship for it. What is't your
worship's pleasure I shall do with this wicked caitiff?

ESCALUS Truly, Officer, because he hath some offenses in him   165
that thou wouldst discover, if thou couldst, let him continue
in his courses till thou know'st what they are.

ELBOW Marry, I thank your worship for it. Thou seest, thou
wicked varlet, now what's come upon thee. Thou art to
continue now, thou varlet, thou art to continue.   170

ESCALUS [*To* FROTH.] Where were you born, friend?

FROTH Here in Vienna, sir.

ESCALUS Are you of fourscore pounds a year?

FROTH Yes, an't please you, sir.

ESCALUS [*To* POMPEY.] So, what trade are you of, sir?   175

POMPEY A tapster, a poor widow's tapster.

ESCALUS Your mistress's name?

POMPEY Mistress Overdone.°

ESCALUS Hath she had any more than one husband?

POMPEY Nine, sir, Overdone by the last.   180

ESCALUS Nine? Come hither to me, Master Froth. Master Froth,
I would not have you acquainted with tapsters, they will

villain

error for "Pompey," another
famous general

the object of Escalus' satire, gratefully accepts the
proposal and believes that he has won his case. This
whole sequence is important for establishing Escalus
as a figure of authority who has compassion, humanity and humor, in contrast to Angelo. In many ways
the play is an essay on power, justice and politics
and this sequence is crucial in production as a parallel to the abuse of power used by Angelo during his
role as judge; it must be funny and warm in tone.

error for "slander"

171-187 Escalus gently interrogates Froth and
Pompey, using a softer tone, introduced by using the
term "friend". Concluding that Froth is naive rather
than guilty of any crime, Escalus sends him off with
parting, paternal words of advice.

i.e., overly sexually practiced

draw° you, Master Froth, and you will hang them.° Get you
gone, and let me hear no more of you.

FROTH   I thank your worship. For mine own part, I never come   185
into any room in a tap-house but I am drawn in.

ESCALUS   Well, no more of it, Master Froth, farewell.
                                                    [*Exit* FROTH.]
Come you hither to me, Master Tapster. What's your name,
Master Tapster?

POMPEY   Pompey.   190

ESCALUS   What else?

POMPEY   Bum, sir.

ESCALUS   Troth, and your bum° is the greatest thing about you,
so that in the beastliest sense, you are Pompey the great.
Pompey, you are partly a bawd,° Pompey, howsoever you   195
color it in being a tapster, are you not? Come, tell me true, it
shall be the better for you.

POMPEY   Truly sir, I am a poor fellow that would live.

ESCALUS   How would you live, Pompey? By being a bawd? What
do you think of the trade, Pompey? Is it a lawful trade?   200

POMPEY   If the law would allow it, sir.

ESCALUS   But the law will not allow it, Pompey, nor it shall not
be allowed in Vienna.

POMPEY   Does your worship mean to geld° and splay° all the
youth of the city?   205

ESCALUS   No, Pompey.

POMPEY   Truly, sir, in my poor opinion they will to't then. If
your worship will take order for the drabs° and the knaves,°
you need not to fear the bawds.

ESCALUS   There is pretty orders beginning, I can tell you. It is   210
but heading° and hanging.

POMPEY   If you head and hang all that offend that way but for
ten year together, you'll be glad to give out a commission for
more heads. If this law hold in Vienna ten year, I'll rent the

draw ale, puns on "lure"
  i.e., help to have them
  hanged

189-226 In this exchange with Pompey, Escalus exhibits again his humanity and good humor as he verbally wrestles with him before letting him off with a warning. Pompey wickedly turns to the audience on his exit and delights in telling them that it will be business as usual (223-225). It is also possible in production to show Pompey actually heading off straight back to business as his low-life friends wait for him and shake his hand in celebration of his release. Throughout this sequence with Froth and Pompey there is additional visual comedy as the luckless Elbow winces and responds to the new turn of events that will set his prisoners free. This sequence is an especially good comic vehicle for the actor playing Pompey and in many productions allows him to demonstrate a swaggering disdain for authority. In Michael Rudman's Caribbean version, for example, Pompey was seen here "as a white-suited rogue, in two-tone shoes, arrogantly parking his bum on the tribunal desk" (*The Guardian*, 15 April 1981).

buttocks

pimp

castrate   spay

prostitutes   base men

beheading

fairest house in it after, three pence a bay.° If you live to   215
see this come to pass, say Pompey told you so.

ESCALUS   Thank you, good Pompey, and in requital of your pro-
phecy, hark you: I advise you let me not find you before me
again upon any complaint whatsoever, no, not for dwelling
where you do. If I do, Pompey, I shall beat you to your tent,   220
and prove a shrewd Caesar° to you. In plain dealing, Pompey, I
shall have you whipped. So for this time, Pompey, fare you well.

POMPEY   I thank your worship for your good counsel, but I shall
follow it as the flesh and fortune shall better determine.
Whip me? No, no let carman whip his jade,° the valiant   225
heart's not whipped out of his trade.   *Exit.*

ESCALUS   Come hither to me, Master Elbow, come hither, Master
Constable. How long have you been in this place of Constable?

ELBOW   Seven year, and a half, sir.

ESCALUS   I thought by the readiness in the office you had   230
continued in it some time. You say seven years together?

ELBOW   And a half, sir.

ESCALUS   Alas, it hath been great pains to you. They do you
wrong to put you so oft upon't. Are there not men in your
ward° sufficient to serve it?   235

ELBOW   'Faith, sir, few of any wit in such matters; as they are
chosen, they are glad to choose me for them. I do it for some
piece of money and go through with all.

ESCALUS   Look you bring me in the names of some six or seven,
the most sufficient of your parish.   240

ELBOW   To your worship's house, sir?

ESCALUS   To my house. Fare you well.   [*Exit* ELBOW *and* OFFICERS.]
What's a clock, think you?

JUSTICE   Eleven, sir.

ESCALUS   I pray you home to dinner with me.   245

JUSTICE   I humbly thank you.

ESCALUS   It grieves me for the death of Claudio,

area

victor of the historical Pompey
in 48 BC

cart-driver whip his horse

district

227-253 Escalus then turns his attentions once again to Elbow, who is confused about what he has just witnessed; his earlier feeling of triumph has evaporated and he has now become downcast. Once again though, Escalus is gentle with him as he gives him a mission that will raise his spirits. Elbow exits (242) in a state of excitement as he dashes off to round up his men.

In contrast, Escalus and the Justice discuss the situation with sad and honest reflections on the fate of Claudio: "It grieves me for the death of Claudio" (247). They have moved closer together for this quiet, private moment and exit into a rare moment of silence in the play with the brief words of Escalus, "Come, sir". The verse-line is left unfinished as the audience has a moment to grasp the reality of the situation for Claudio. This moment is important due to the speed of change backwards and forwards between broad comedy and tragedy throughout the play. It is essential that the execution appears as a real possibility and is separated from the comic sub-plot; if this is not achieved the dramatic tension of the play collapses.

But there's no remedy.

JUSTICE   Lord Angelo is severe.

ESCALUS   It is but needful.
Mercy is not itself that oft looks so,   250
Pardon is still the nurse of second woe.
But yet, poor Claudio, there is no remedy.
Come, sir.   *Exeunt.*

Scene ii   *Enter* PROVOST *and a* SERVANT.

SERVANT   He's hearing of a cause,° he will come straight,
I'll tell him of you.

PROVOST   'Pray you do.   [*Exit* SERVANT.]
                                         I'll know
His pleasure, maybe he will relent. Alas,
He° hath but as offended in a dream;
All sects, all ages, smack of this vice, and he   5
To die for't?

                    Enter ANGELO.

ANGELO   Now, what's the matter, Provost?

PROVOST   Is it your will Claudio shall die tomorrow?

ANGELO   Did not I tell thee yea? Hast thou not order?
Why dost thou ask again?

PROVOST   Lest I might be too rash.
Under your good correction, I have seen   10
When after execution, judgement hath
Repented o'er his doom.

ANGELO   Go to, let that be mine,
Do you your office, or give up your place,°
And you shall well be spared.

Scene ii

1-6   The scene begins with the entrance of the
Provost and a servant and is clearly located in the
palace where Angelo is based. The setting, however,
is more intimate than in previous scenes and is perhaps located in private chambers rather than a large,
open space. The Provost has asked the servant to
bring Angelo to talk with him; the servant indicates
that Angelo is busy and suggests that he had to be
case   interrupted and this helps to explain the curtness of
Angelo's tone with the Provost. The Provost is
allowed a few seconds alone on the stage to establish an understanding with the audience (3-6). It is
significant that, like Escalus before him (II.i.247), the
Provost makes it clear that he has sympathy for
Claudio and feels the punishment to be unjust. His
Claudio   short soliloquy is interrupted by Angelo's arrival,
announced by the blunt, contrapuntal "Now, what's
the matter, Provost"; Angelo is impatient from his
arrival and is anxious to get on with his business.

7-14   Angelo is probably not giving much attention to the Provost and is continuing with business of
state throughout this exchange. He might be finishing
the signed warrant for Claudio's death referred to
later in the play (IV.ii.55). He may sit at a large desk
and continue reading and signing documents as they
speak. The Provost hesitantly tries to draw Angelo's
attention with the long verse-line "Is it your will
Claudio shall die tomorrow?" The lingering finality of
"tomorrow" is emphasised by the feminine ending, as
the Provost nervously questions Angelo's command.
Angelo is indeed distracted from other business and
snaps back at him that he has no right to question his
commands. The Provost, uncowed, immediately continues his mission and, jumping on the half verse-line
of Angelo he presses his case (9). Angelo's response
is again harsh and this time final as he reaffirms his
intentions and threatens the Provost with "Do you
position   your office, or give up your place" (13). This time the
Provost recognises defeat and rapidly finishes another half-verse line of Angelo's, but this time with an
apology: "I crave your honor's pardon." The Provost

PROVOST   I crave your honor's pardon.
  What shall be done, sir, with the groaning° Juliet?   15
  She's very near her hour.°

ANGELO   Dispose of her
  To some more fitter place, and that with speed.

[Enter SERVANT.*]*

SERVANT   Here is the sister of the man condemned
  Desires access to you.

ANGELO   Hath he a sister?

PROVOST   Aye, my good lord, a very virtuous maid,   20
  And to be shortly of a sisterhood,
  If not already.

ANGELO   Well, let her be admitted.   *[Exit* SERVANT.*]*
  [To PROVOST.*]* See you the fornicatress be removed,
  Let her have needful but not lavish means,
  There shall be order for't.

Enter LUCIO *and* ISABELLA.

PROVOST   'Save your honor.   25

ANGELO   Stay a little while. *[To* ISABELLA.*]* You're welcome.
  What's your will?

ISABELLA   I am a woeful suitor to your honor,
  'Please but your honor hear me.

ANGELO   Well, what's your suit?

ISABELLA   There is a vice that most I do abhor,   30
  And most desire should meet the blow of justice,
  For which I would not plead, but that I must,
  For which I must not plead, but that I am
  At war twixt will and will not.

ANGELO   Well, the matter?

ISABELLA   I have a brother is condemned to die;   35
  I do beseech you, let it be his fault,

i.e., in labor

hour of giving birth

changes his body language and tone as he backs off when confronted by this warning. This whole sequence is a prelude to the arrival of Isabella, as the audience witnesses the apparent, rigid certitude that Angelo exhibits, even in the face of passionate objections of the men around him.

14-24 The Provost brings the world of women into the hitherto very male world of Angelo and his officials by his reference to the pregnant Juliet. Angelo is unwilling to be drawn into this world and dismissively waves his arm and tells the Provost to get rid of her "to some more fitter place" (18). A servant enters and announces the arrival of another woman: Claudio's sister Isabella. Angelo expresses surprise at hearing that he has a sister, as though he has never really thought about Claudio as an individual with a family and a normal life. This expression of surprise seems to suggest a momentary flicker of awareness that Claudio is not just a symbol of a lawbreaker and a convenient object with which to demonstrate the power of the new laws. The Provost cleverly capitalizes on this almost imperceptible stirring and adds rapidly that Isabella is, or is about to become a nun. Angelo agrees to meet her and sends the Provost off on his mission to deal with Juliet.

25-42 The timing of the entrance of Lucio and Isabella is important and follows on exactly between the end of Angelo's command "There shall be order for't" and the Provost's response "save your honor." (25). As these two phrases are part of a shared verse line the indication is that Angelo sees Isabella precisely at this point, as the Provost is beginning his exit.

On seeing Isabella, Angelo immediately changes his mind and commands the Provost to stay. He probably stands up and seems to feel a sudden and strong reaction to her presence, even though they have not yet spoken with each other. It is as though he feels an immediate and extreme, yet inexplicable, sense of weakness as he looks at her and so decides to keep the Provost there as both a witness and a reminder to him of his duty. It is a strange and powerful moment on the stage even before the dialogue begins. Isabella herself senses something from Angelo at this moment and refers back to it near the end of the play (V.i.438). As is so often the case in Shakespeare's plays, especially during verse sequences, emotions and passions begin immediately and then evolve and develop rapidly within a short space of time. As Isabella begins her pleading, Angelo recovers control and

And not my brother.

PROVOST   [*Aside.*]   Heaven give thee moving graces!

ANGELO   Condemn the fault and not the actor of it?
Why every fault's condemned ere it be done.
Mine were the very cipher of a function°   40
To fine the faults, whose fine stands in record,
And let go by the actor.

ISABELLA   O just, but severe law!
I had a brother then. Heaven keep your honor.

LUCIO   [*Aside to* ISABELLA.] Give't not o'er so. To him again,
    entreat him,
Kneel down before him, hang upon his gown,   45
You are too cold. If you should need a pin,
You could not with more tame a tongue desire it.
To him, I say.

ISABELLA   [*To* ANGELO.] Must he needs die?

ANGELO   Maiden, no remedy.

ISABELLA   Yes, I do think that you might pardon him,   50
And neither heaven nor man grieve at the mercy.

ANGELO   I will not do't.

ISABELLA   But can you if you would?

ANGELO   Look what I will not, that I cannot do.

ISABELLA   But might you do't and do the world no wrong,
If so your heart were touched with that remorse   55
As mine is to him?

ANGELO   He's sentenced, 'tis too late.

LUCIO   [*Aside to* ISABELLA.] You are too cold.

ISABELLA   Too late? Why no, I that do speak a word
May call it again. Well believe this:
No ceremony that to great ones longs,   60
Not the king's crown, nor the deputed sword,
The marshal's truncheon,° nor the judge's robe
Become them with one half so good a grace

cuts her off abruptly, in the middle of a verse-line with the blunt "Well, what's your suit" (28). Perhaps he sits down again behind the protection of his large desk, as Isabella lyrically and obliquely begins her appeal (29-33). Whilst she is determined to open up a moral and complex debate, Angelo tries hard to keep a business-like tone to the encounter and again finishes her final verse line with another interruption preceded by the gruff "well, the matter." Isabella responds by a more direct form of words as she approaches Angelo and asks him to continue condemning the actions but to allow mercy to her brother who has committed those actions.

empty symbol of office

Whilst for a moment Angelo muses on this apparent contradiction, the Provost, probably positioned close to the audience, has time for a brief aside as he prays for her success. Angelo finds himself drawn into the debate for a moment as his bemused response rejects her curious argument. Isabella accepts defeat and moves away toward the exit, where Lucio is waiting (42).

43-48   Angelo is left alone, perhaps surprised that he has been touched in some way by this brief encounter, as Lucio grabs Isabella and urges her to try harder to get through to Angelo. By instinct, Lucio knows that Angelo is feeling something from Isabella and his street-wise understanding of men makes him advise Isabella that she must come physically close to Angelo and raise the emotional temperature of the meeting: "Kneel down before him, hang upon his gown" (45).

Isabella decides to try again and crosses back to Angelo, who is perhaps by now standing in the middle of the stage. She may or may not actually kneel at his feet as Lucio has advised; this probably happens later in the scene, but either way the tone clearly suggests more intimacy as Isabella argues simply that Angelo can if he wishes pardon Claudio. Each time Angelo says no Isabella continues to urge her case as though trying to wear him down. If she is indeed not kneeling at his feet and clutching his robes then she is probably pursuing him around the room as he tries, in vain, to end the discussion.

All the time the Provost and Lucio are reacting as they watch the performance between Angelo and Isabella take place before them.

staff of office

56-90   Isabella becomes increasingly eloquent and passionate as she searches for more arguments and is urged on by whispered encouragements from Lucio (57 and 71). Although according to the modern

    As mercy does. If he had been as you, and you as he,
    You would have slipped like him, but he like you   65
    Would not have been so stern.

ANGELO   Pray you be gone.

ISABELLA   I would to heaven I had your potency,
    And you were Isabell. Should it then be thus?
    No, I would tell what 'twere to be a judge,
    And what a prisoner.   70

LUCIO   [*Aside to* ISABELLA.] Aye, touch him, there's the vein.

ANGELO   Your brother is a forfeit of the law,
    And you but waste your words.

ISABELLA   Alas, alas!
    Why all the souls that were, were forfeit once,
    And he that might the vantage° best have took   75
    Found out the remedy. How would you be,
    If he, which is the top of judgement, should
    But judge you as you are? Oh, think on that,
    And mercy then will breathe within your lips
    Like man new-made.

ANGELO   Be you content, fair maid,   80
    It is the law, not I, condemn your brother.
    Were he my kinsman, brother, or my son,
    It should be thus with him: he must die tomorrow.

ISABELLA   Tomorrow? Oh, that's sudden! Spare him, spare him!
    He's not prepared for death; even for our kitchens   85
    We kill the fowl of season. Shall we serve heaven
    With less respect then we do minister
    To our gross selves? Good, good my lord, bethink you:
    Who is it that hath died for this offence?
    There's many have committed it.

LUCIO   [*Aside to* ISABELLA.]   Aye, well said.   90

ANGELO   The law hath not been dead, though it hath slept.
    Those many had not dared to do that evil
    If the first that did th'edict infringe
    Had answered for his deed. Now 'tis awake,
    Takes note of what is done, and like a prophet   95

editor's stage directions these are asides to Isabella, it is also possible to stage the scene with Lucio not so close to her, in effect playing the asides to the audience.

In spite of the fact that Angelo repeatedly refuses to accept any possibility of a change of mind, he seems powerless to stop the pleading and berating from Isabella, as she continually challenges him to show mercy. The tension of the scene accelerates when Angelo reinforces the command that Claudio must die "tomorrow" (83). As she hears the word "tomorrow" Isabella cries out, with the greatest emotion so far in the scene, "spare him, Spare him" (84). It is perhaps at this point that Isabella kneels at his feet and grasps his robes as referred to near the end of the play (V.i.93). This physical contact is a crucial moment for defining the reaction of Angelo to Isabella. In some productions he remains icily indifferent to her whereas in others it is the first moment that the audience sees the intense sexual feelings within Angelo, triggered by her touch.

advantage

    Looks in a glass° that shows what future evils—
    Either now, or by remissness, new conceived,
    And so in progress to be hatched and born—
    Are now to have no successive degrees,
    But here they live to end.

ISABELLA   Yet show some pity.   100

ANGELO   I show it most of all when I show justice,
    For then I pity those I do not know,
    Which a dismissed offense would after gall
    And do him right, that answering one foul wrong
    Lives not to act another. Be satisfied.   105
    Your brother dies tomorrow. Be content.

ISABELLA   So you must be the first that gives this sentence,
    And he that suffers. Oh it is excellent
    To have a giant's strength, but it is tyrannous
    To use it like a giant.   110

LUCIO   [*Aside to* ISABELLA.] That's well said.

ISABELLA   Could great men thunder
    As Jove himself does, Jove would never be quiet,
    For every pelting,° petty officer
    Would use his heaven for thunder,   115
    Nothing but thunder. Merciful heaven,
    Thou rather with thy sharp and sulphurous bolt
    Splits the unwedgeable and gnarlèd oak
    Than the soft myrtle. But man, proud man,
    Dressed in a little brief authority,   120
    Most ignorant of what he's most assured,
    His glassy essence,° like an angry ape
    Plays such fantastic tricks before high heaven
    As makes the angels weep, who with our spleens°
    Would all themselves laugh mortal.   125

LUCIO   [*Aside to* ISABELLA.] Oh, to him, to him wench. He will relent,
    He's coming, I perceive't.

PROVOST   [*Aside.*]   Pray heaven she win him.

ISABELLA   We cannot weigh our brother with ourself.

mirror

paltry

transparent soul

seats of mirth or melancholy

107-145 During the increasingly complex theological exchanges Isabella repeatedly personalizes the situation in order to force Angelo to examine his conscience. She suggests that he is behaving like a petty tyrant (109 and 120), thereby cueing the audience in the theatre to do the same. As she tries desperately to move him in some way, Lucio, almost taking on the role of chorus as he comments on the action, indicates that something about Angelo's reactions suggests that he is beginning to weaken under the storm of emotions and arguments unleashed on him by Isabella: "He's coming, I perceive't" (127). The Provost joins in with his own aside, following on from Lucio's. Angelo is now silent until line 135, whilst Isabella presses her attack and Lucio continues his asides. During this short gap, Angelo might change his stage position as an attempt to retreat from Isabella; a few lines later (145), he tries to exit from the scene. Just before this moment, for the first time in the scene, Angelo verbalizes to the audience his anguish as he recognizes that she has touched him with her words (144).

Great men may jest with saints, 'tis wit in them,
But in the less, foul prophanation.   130

LUCIO   [*Aside to* ISABELLA.] Thou'rt i'th'right, girl, more o'that.

ISABELLA   That in the captain's but a choleric° word
Which in the soldier is flat blasphemy.

LUCIO   [*Aside to* ISABELLA.] Art avised o'that? More on't.

ANGELO   Why do you put these sayings upon me?   135

ISABELLA   Because authority, though it err like others,
Hath yet a kind of medicine in itself
That skins° the vice o'th' top. Go to your bosom,
Knock there, and ask your heart what it doth know
That's like my brother's fault. If it confess   140
A natural guiltiness, such as is his,
Let it not sound a thought upon your tongue
Against my brother's life.

ANGELO   [*Aside.*] She speaks, and 'tis such sense
That my sense° breeds with it. [*To* ISABELLA.] Fare you well.   145

ISABELLA   Gentle my lord, turn back!

ANGELO   I will bethink me. Come again tomorrow.

ISABELLA   Hark how I'll bribe you! Good my lord, turn back.

ANGELO   How? Bribe me?

ISABELLA   Aye, with such gifts that heaven shall share with you.   150

LUCIO   [*Aside to* ISABELLA.] You had marred all, else.

ISABELLA   Not with fond sickles° of the tested gold,
Or stones, whose rate are either rich or poor
As fancy values them, but with true prayers,
That shall be up at heaven and enter there   155
Ere sunrise, prayers from preservèd souls,
From fasting maids, whose minds are dedicate°
To nothing temporal.

ANGELO   Well, come to me tomorrow.

LUCIO   [*Aside to* ISABELLA.] Go to, 'tis well, away.

angry

skims

sensuality

coins

dedicated

146-164 However, just as he is on the point of exiting and has his back to all in the room, Angelo hears softly spoken words behind him: "Gentle my lord, turn back" (146).

With his back still turned toward her Angelo hesitates in the silence that follows this unfinished verse-line and then offers the first hint of any hope for Claudio as he quietly responds with "I will bethink me. Come again tomorrow". Isabella continues with this new gentler tone as she offers to "bribe" Angelo tomorrow. He turns around in surprise at these words he does not know how to interpret. The suspicions in his mind are echoed for the audience by Lucio who assumes the ambiguity is deliberate, as he congratulates Isabella on the idea: "You had marred all else" (151). Isabella seems oblivious of possible sexual innuendo or double meanings concerning material bribes, although it is possible to play the character with more instinctive knowing, as she goes on to explain about the prayers that she is referring to (154).

Angelo tries to recover his calm and returns to the tone of the beginning of the scene with another blunt, "Well, come to me tomorrow." As Isabella and Lucio begin to exit with her line "Heaven keep your honour safe," Angelo finishes the verse-

ISABELLA   Heaven keep your honor safe.

ANGELO   [*Aside.*]   Amen,   160
    For I am that way going to temptation,
    Where prayers cross.

ISABELLA   At what hour tomorrow
    Shall I attend your lordship?

ANGELO   At any time 'fore noon.

ISABELLA   Save° your honour.   [*Exeunt all but* ANGELO.]

ANGELO   From thee, even from thy virtue.
    What's this? What's this? is this her fault, or mine?   165
    The tempter, or the tempted, who sins most? Ha?
    Not she, nor doth she tempt, but it is I
    That, lying by the violet° in the sun,
    Do as the carrion° does, not as the flower,
    Corrupt with virtuous season. Can it be   170
    That modesty may more betray our sense
    Than woman's lightness°? Having waste ground enough,
    Shall we desire to raze the sanctuary
    And pitch our evils there? Oh fie, fie, fie!
    What dost thou, or what art thou, Angelo?   175
    Dost thou desire her foully for those things
    That make her good? Oh, let her brother live!
    Thieves for their robbery have authority
    When judges steal themselves. What, do I love her,
    That I desire to hear her speak again   180
    And feast upon her eyes? What is't I dream on?
    Oh cunning enemy, that to catch a saint,
    With saints dost bait thy hook! Most dangerous
    Is that temptation that doth goad us on
    To sin in loving virtue. Never could the strumpet   185
    With all her double° vigor, art, and nature
    Once stir my temper, but this virtuous maid
    Subdues me quite. Ever till now
    When men were fond,° I smiled, and wondered how.   *Exit.*

line with the one word "Amen" (160), and then turns to the audience to confess his weakness in the face of temptation. Isabella and Lucio finish their exit agreeing with Angelo that she will come tomorrow before noon (163). The Provost, seeing the dark expression on Angelo's face, quickly exits after the other two.

God save

165-189 Left alone at last on the stage, Angelo shares his thoughts with the audience as he anguishes over the recognition that he cannot resist the desires that Isabella has awoken in him. This can also be a moment when the audience begins to understand the full, dark consequences of this scene that must now follow. In David Thacker's production, for example, the moment was emphasized as Angelo "slowly removes his glasses with a Hitchcockian sense of slow menace to disclose unblinking eyes" (*The Guardian*, 19 April 1989).

The speech ends with Angelo leaving the stage, perplexed and confused.

symbol of purity
corpse

wantonness

deceitful

infatuated

Scene iii   *Enter* DUKE *[disguised as a Friar] and* PROVOST.

DUKE   Hail to you, Provost, so I think you are.

PROVOST   I am the Provost. What's your will, good Friar?

DUKE   Bound by my charity and my blest order,
I come to visit the afflicted spirits
Here in the prison. Do me the common right   5
To let me see them and to make me know
The nature of their crimes, that I may minister
To them accordingly.

PROVOST   I would do more than that if more were needful.

Enter JULIET.

Look here comes one, a gentlewoman of mine,   10
Who falling in the flaws of her own youth,
Hath blistered her report.° She is with child,
And he that got° it sentenced; a young man
More fit to do another such offense
Than die for this.   15

DUKE   When must he die?

PROVOST   As I do think, tomorrow.
[*To* JULIET.] I have provided for you; stay a while
And you shall be conducted.

DUKE   Repent you, fair one, of the sin you carry?   20

JULIET   I do, and bear the shame most patiently.

DUKE   I'll teach you how you shall arraign your conscience
And try your penitence, if it be sound
Or hollowly put on.

JULIET   I'll gladly learn.   25

DUKE   Love you the man that wronged you?

Scene iii

1-18   The scene takes place in the prison area underneath the palace. The Duke, now in disguise, enters and meets the Provost who has entered from the opposite direction, coming from Angelo's chamber in the last scene. The Duke, not yet accustomed to his disguise, calls out a greeting to the Provost, but suddenly remembering that he is not supposed to know who he is, covers his tracks with "so I think you are." This element of gentle humor nearly always remains with the Duke in the play, especially while he remains in disguise, and it is possible to interpret his character in a way that shows him to be an accidentally comic character who is constantly making errors of judgment like this. He can be seen as an incompetent ruler, out of his depth, who has made such a mess of his job that he must let someone else sort it out.

In many productions the use of disguise causes problems for modern audiences, especially, apparently, in director John Pasquin's production in New York's Central Park where the Duke " tosses his Friar's hood on and off his head so many times...that it finally becomes a subject of unintentional humour" (*The New York Times*, 13 August 1976). Most directors simply accept the disguise as a convention and do not attempt a detailed, realistic hiding of the Duke's identity, as in director Adrian Noble's production: "but it does take a bit of swallowing to believe he would have fooled some of his oldest retainers into believing he was a simple monk without bothering to wear any disguise, except for an on-and-off cowl" (*Evening Standard*, 18 April 1984).

As the Duke begins to find appropriate language for his new persona Juliet enters (9). She enters from a point a distance away from the two men so that the Provost has enough time to quickly explain her situation to the Duke before she has joined them (10-17). This time gap is important in order to allow the full reaction of shock from Juliet some lines later when Angelo tells her that Claudio will die tomorrow (39). As he tells the story the Provost makes a point of expressing his negative opinion of the sentence (14).

i.e., ruined her reputation
begot

26-41   The Duke takes Juliet to one side as he

JULIET   Yes, as I love the woman that wronged him.

DUKE   So then it seems your most offenseful act
    Was mutually committed.

JULIET   Mutually.

DUKE   Then was your sin of heavier kind than his.   30

JULIET   I do confess it, and repent it, Father.

DUKE   'Tis meet so, daughter, but lest you do repent
    As that the sin hath brought you to this shame,
    Which sorrow is always toward ourselves, not heaven,
    Showing we would not spare heaven as we love it,   35
    But as we stand in fear—

JULIET   I do repent me as it is an evil,
    And take the shame with joy.

DUKE   There rest.
    Your partner, as I hear, must die tomorrow,
    And I am going with instruction to him.   40
    Grace go with you; *Benedicite.*°   *Exit.*

JULIET   Must die tomorrow? O injurious love
    That respites me a life, whose very comfort
    Is still a dying horror!

PROVOST   'Tis pity of him.   *Exeunt.*

Scene iv   *Enter* ANGELO.

ANGELO   When I would pray, and think, I think, and pray
    To several subjects. Heaven hath my empty words,
    Whilst my invention, hearing not my tongue,
    Anchors on Isabel: heaven in my mouth,
    As if I did but only chew his name,   5
    And in my heart the strong and swelling evil
    Of my conception. The state whereon I studied
    Is like a good thing, being often read,

interrogates her about whether or not she repents what she has done. The Duke takes her hand, perhaps, as he directly asks her if she loves Claudio. Instead of an automatic answer, she takes a moment after the Duke's unfinished verse-line, to look him in the eyes before answering, clearly, slowly and nobly answering, "Yes, as I love the woman that wronged him" (27). In this reply and throughout this short exchange Juliet always accepts full blame and responsibility for the situation. The Duke brings the meeting to a rapid end as he exits to seek out Claudio. The scene ends with Juliet in emotional turmoil as she realises that Claudio will die tomorrow and the Provost expresses pity. This note of tragic sadness is still hanging in the air as the lights, in a modern theatre, would indicate to us it is night and a long day is over.

Bless you

Scene iv

1-30 It is now morning and we find Angelo alone in his chamber, in the middle of debating with himself the evil of the desire for Isabella that he is feeling. It is possible that he has in fact been up all night, haunted by these thoughts that we hear part of as the scene opens. He starts nervously as he hears a servant approach, almost as though he is afraid that his unspoken, dark thoughts will be overheard. As the servant is sent away to bring in Isabella, Angelo continues to work himself up into a frenzy of emotion before she arrives.

Grown seared° and tedious. Yea, my gravity,
Wherein, let no man hear me, I take pride,   10
Could I, with boot,° change for an idle plume
Which the air beats for vain. Oh place,° oh form,°
How often dost thou with thy case, thy habit,
Wrench awe from fools and tie the wiser souls
To thy false seeming? Blood, thou art blood!   15
Let's write 'good angel' on the devil's horn,
'Tis not the devil's crest. How now? Who's there?

Enter SERVANT.

SERVANT   One Isabel, a sister, desires access to you.

ANGELO   Teach her the way.   [*Exit* SERVANT.]
                        O heavens,
Why does my blood thus muster to my heart,   20
Making both it unable for itself
And dispossessing all my other parts
Of necessary fitness?
So play the foolish throngs with one that swoons,
Come all to help him, and so stop the air   25
By which he should revive; and even so
The general subject to a well-wished° king
Quit their own part, and in obsequious fondness
Crowd to his presence, where their untaught love
Must needs appear offense.

Enter ISABELLA.

                        How now, fair maid?   30

ISABELLA   I am come to know your pleasure.

ANGELO   [*Aside.*] That you might know it would much better please
     me,
     Than to demand what 'tis. [*To* ISABELLA.] Your brother
     cannot live.

ISABELLA   Even so. Heaven keep your honor.

ANGELO   Yet may he live a while, and it may be   35
     As long as you, or I, yet he must die.

dried up

advantage
exalted position   noble
  behavior

recipient of the people's good
  wishes

31-87 As she enters and stands before Angelo, Isabella's first line is accidentally loaded with exactly those sexual connotations that have haunted him all night. It is as though she is declaring that she has come to do whatever he desires, although the actual meaning is innocent (31). However, the ambiguity of her words provokes a tormented aside by Angelo as he tells us that he would prefer her to offer what he really wants rather than his having to say what it is. There is a humor within the tensions of all this as the audience is drawn into Angelo's secret thoughts by his asides. At the end of the aside (33) Angelo tries

ISABELLA   Under your sentence?

ANGELO   Yea.

ISABELLA   When, I beseech you? That in his reprieve,
    Longer or shorter, he may be so fitted°   40
    That his soul sicken not.

ANGELO   Ha? Fie, these filthy vices! It were as good
    To pardon him, that hath from nature stolen
    A man already made, as to remit
    Their saucy° sweetness that do coin heaven's image   45
    In stamps that are forbid. 'Tis all as easy
    Falsely to take away a life true-made
    As to put metal in restrainèd means°
    To make a false one.

ISABELLA   'Tis set down so in heaven, but not in earth.   50

ANGELO   Say you so? Then I shall pose° you quickly.
    Which had you rather: that the most just law
    Now took your brother's life, or, to redeem him,
    Give up your body to such sweet uncleanness
    As she that he hath stained?

ISABELLA   Sir, believe this: 55
    I had rather give my body than my soul.

ANGELO   I talk not of your soul. Our compellèd sins
    Stand more for number than for accompt.°

ISABELLA   How say you?

ANGELO   Nay, I'll not warrant that, for I can speak
    Against the thing I say. Answer to this: 60
    I, now the voice of the recorded law,
    Pronounce a sentence on your brother's life;
    Might there not be a charity in sin
    To save this brother's life?

ISABELLA   Please you to do't,
    I'll take it as a peril to my soul,   65
    It is no sin at all, but charity.

ANGELO   Pleased you to do't, at peril of your soul,
    Were equal poise of sin and charity.

to get down to business with the simple and brutal
statement "Your brother cannot live". Isabella is not
drawn by this and takes the high ground and probably begins to exit with careful choice of the words
"Heaven" and "honor", echoing the themes of the
previous scene between them both. Angelo quickly
throws out a carrot to keep her there, as he suggests
that there could be a reprieve. Isabella stops dead in
her tracks as she tries to interpret Angelo's ambiguous words and in her short, challenging response
she tries to clarify whether Claudio will or will not be
executed (37). After a telling silence, he responds
coldly and starkly "Yea." Isabella takes this to mean
that Angelo is talking about a delay of execution
rather than a reprieve.

prepared

wanton

i.e., to counterfeit coins

question

51-73   Angelo strives to get closer to his theme as
he poses the question to Isabella about whether she
would sacrifice her own virtues by indulging in sex if
that would allow the greater virtue of saving her
brother's life (51-55). Isabella appears not to understand the challenge and returns to the theme of
mercy as she again tries to convince Angelo that it
would not be sinful for him to save her brother: "It is
no sin at all but charity" (66). Throughout the whole
scene there is a significant difference in mood and
situation to those in their previous encounter: They
are now alone and Angelo is free to come as close as
he wishes and to employ unguarded language. He
must feel more dangerous this time as he stalks
Isabella before moving in for the kill. The physical
movement of the scene probably reflects this verbal
circling as Angelo endeavours to make Isabella
understand what he is proposing. There are almost
no specific references within the text to the physical
staging of this scene and Shakespeare's intentions
must be gleaned from subtle shifts of mood and tone
throughout their encounter.

account

ISABELLA   That I do beg his life, if it be sin,
          Heaven let me bear it. You granting of my suit,   70
          It that be sin, I'll make it my morn° prayer
          To have it added to the faults of mine
          And nothing of your answer.

ANGELO   Nay, but hear me,
          Your sense pursues not mine. Either you are ignorant,
          Or seem so craftily, and that's not good.   75

ISABELLA   Let me be ignorant, and in nothing good,
          But graciously to know I am no better.

ANGELO   Thus wisdom wishes to appear most bright
          When it doth tax itself, as these black masks
          Proclaim an en-shield° beauty ten times louder   80
          Than beauty could displayed. But mark me,
          To be received plain, I'll speak more gross:°
          Your brother is to die.

ISABELLA   So.

ANGELO   And his offence is so, as it appears,   85
          Accountant to the law upon that pain.

ISABELLA   True.

ANGELO   Admit no other way to save his life—
          As I subscribe not that, nor any other—
          But in the loss of question, that you, his sister,   90
          Finding yourself desired of such a person
          Whose credit with the judge, or own great place,
          Could fetch your brother from the manacles
          Of the all-binding law, and that there were
          No earthly mean to save him, but that either   95
          You must lay down the treasures of your body
          To this supposed, or else to let him suffer;
          What would you do?

ISABELLA   As much for my poor brother as myself;
          That is, were I under the terms of death,   100
          Th'impression of keen whips I'd wear as rubies,
          And strip myself to death, as to a bed
          That longing have been sick for, ere I'd yield

morning

shielded

obviously

74-124   Angelo expresses his frustration that Isabella does not seem to grasp his meaning and suspects her of feigning innocence (74); he changes again the tone and language as he moves in for the kill and explains the bargain he is offering. He is now physically close to Isabella and perhaps holds her fast as he gives his ultimatum that she "must lay down the treasures of your body" if she wishes to save her brother's life (96).

After Angelo's taunting half line "What would you do?" (98), there is a silence before Isabella responds, and she takes a deep breath before bursting out with a passionate and angry response (99-104). This is in contrast to Angelo's. very dispassionate and clinical, curt reply, "Then must your brother die" (105). Angelo continues to, in effect, circle around his prey as he mocks and tries to provoke her with further taunts, ending the sequence with the meaningful phrase "Nay, women are frail too" (124).

My body up to shame.

ANGELO   Then must your brother die.   105

ISABELLA   And 'twere the cheaper way.
Better it were a brother died at once,
Than that a sister by redeeming him
Should die forever.

ANGELO   Were not you then as cruel as the sentence   110
That you have slandered so?

ISABELLA   Ignomy in ransom° and free pardon
Are of two houses°; lawful mercy
Is nothing kin to foul redemption.

ANGELO   You seemed of late to make the law a tyant,   115
And rather proved the sliding of your brother
A merriment than a vice.

ISABELLA   Oh pardon me, my lord, it oft falls out
To have what we would have, we speak not what we mean.
I something do excuse the thing I hate   120
For his advantage that I dearly love.

ANGELO   We are all frail.

ISABELLA   Else let my brother die,
If not a fedary° but only he
Owe and succeed thy weakness.

ANGELO   Nay, women are frail too.

ISABELLA   Aye, as the glasses° where they view themselves,   125
Which are as easy broke as they make forms.
Women? Help heaven! Men their creation mar
In profiting by them. Nay, call us ten times frail,
For we are soft as our complexions are,
And credulous to false prints.°

ANGELO   I think it well,   130
And from this testimony of your own sex,
Since I suppose we are made to be no stronger
Than faults may shake our frames, let me be bold;
I do arrest your words. Be that you are,
That is, a woman; if you be more, you're none.   135

ransom purchased from
  ignominy or shame
groups

accomplice

mirrors

impressions

132-145 After continuing with his theme of the frailty
of women Angelo finishes his point by challenging
Isabella to be that frail woman and give in to his proposal (138). Isabella changes tone then, as she tries
to control her anger. With gentle irony she begs him

If you be one, as you are well expressed
By all external warrants,° show it now
By putting on the destined livery.°

ISABELLA   I have no tongue but one; gentle my lord,
Let me entreat you speak the former language.   140

ANGELO   Plainly conceive, I love you.

ISABELLA   My brother did love Juliet,
And you tell me that he shall die for't.

ANGELO   He shall not, Isabel, if you give me love.

ISABELLA   I know your virtue hath a license in't,   145
Which seems a little fouler than it is,
To pluck on others.

ANGELO   Believe me on mine honor,
My words express my purpose.

ISABELLA   Ha? Little honor to be much believed,
And most pernicious purpose. Seeming,° seeming!   150
I will proclaim thee, Angelo, look for't!
Sign me a present pardon for my brother,
Or with an out-stretched throat I'll tell the world aloud
What man thou art!

ANGELO   Who will believe thee, Isabel?
My unsoiled name, th'austereness° of my life,   155
My vouch° against you, and my place i'th' state,
Will so your accusation overweigh
That you shall stifle in your own report
And smell of calumny.° I have begun,
And now I give my sensual race the rein.   160
Fit thy consent to my sharp appetite,
Lay by all nicety° and prolixious° blushes
That banish what they sue° for. Redeem thy brother
By yielding up thy body to my will,
Or else he must not only die the death,   165
But thy unkindness shall his death draw out
To ling'ring sufferance. Answer me tomorrow,
Or by the affection that now guides me most,
I'll prove a tyrant to him. As for you,

signs
i.e., a woman's clothing

to stop this theme and behave and speak as he used to (139-140). Angelo seizes the opportunity of this momentary quietness and clumsily declares his love, as he moves in closer to Isabella. On stage there are often two extreme ways of presenting this confrontation: some productions, notably that by director Trevor Nunn at The Young Vic, show Angelo physically attacking and almost raping Isabella "manhandling her like a rapist in a park" (*The Times*, 12 March 1992). Other versions depict Angelo as a cold, unimpassioned man unable to understand anything about physical desire, as in director Jonathan Miller's production where the actor's "prim, fastidious Angelo, expressionless behind his gold-rimmed glasses, makes his tentative and embarrassed passes at Isabel" (*New Statesman*, 30 November 1973) and in Steven Pimlott's production where Angelo was more turned on by power than the idea of sex itself: "less like a lover than a man who, having dipped a toe into duplicity, is seized by the desire to dive in." (*Evening Standard*, 8 June 1995).

Isabella throws back the word "love" (142) and relates it to that of her brother for Juliet. Angelo, unperturbed, presses his case.

falsity

150-171 Angelo's use of the word "honor" (149) is a red rag to a bull and provokes an explosion of contempt and rage from Isabella as she screams out threats to expose him. She too, however, demonstrates how she is capable of blackmail as she offers silence in exchange for a deal for her brother (153-154). Angelo remains icy cool as he mocks her threats and dismisses them contemptuously. He has clearly prepared for this eventuality and his cold, unflinching demand for sex from Isabella is starkly made clear to her. He caps her attempt at blackmail with his own, dark threat to make her brother suffer as much as possible. In this way the scene reaches a climax as the two unmovable, equally determined forces meet in collision. Angelo exits as Isabella is left alone on stage. (170).

severe self-restraint
declaration

slander

modesty   tediously long
plead

Say what you can; my false o'er-weighs your true.   *Exit.* 170

ISABELLA   To whom should I complain? Did I tell this,
Who would believe me? O perilous mouths
That bear in them one and the selfsame tongue,
Either of condemnation or approof,°
Bidding the law make curtsy to their will,   175
Hooking both right and wrong to th'appetite,
To follow as it draws! I'll to my brother;
Though he hath fallen by prompture° of the blood,
Yet hath he in him such a mind of honor
That had he twenty heads to tender down   180
On twenty bloody blocks, he'd yield them up
Before his sister should her body stoop
To such abhorred pollution.
Then Isabel, live chaste, and brother, die;
More than our brother is our chastity.   185
I'll tell him yet of Angelo's request,
And fit his mind to death, for his soul's rest.   *Exit.*

approval

prompting

171-187 Isabella expresses her despair to the audience within the first lines of this soliloquy. She then feels heartened, naively, that her brother will be honorable and prefer to die to save her chastity. Within this belief, one of the central themes of the play is laid out to the audience as Act II comes to an end: Is the chastity of one woman worth the life of one man? To an Elizabethan audience, steeped in an ever-present religious culture, the question is complex and perplexing; to most modern audiences, at least within a Western cultural environment, the answer is perhaps clear and Isabella receives little sympathy for her final decision to let her brother die, "More than our brother is our chastity" (186). Indeed, this is a line that might well be cut in a production today to avoid alienating the audience unnecessarily from Isabella, or, perhaps, spoken in a pained whisper as by Judi Dench in John Blatchley's 1962 production. With a positive belief that Claudio will gladly support her resolve she exits from the stage with a strangely upbeat final rhyming couplet as she sets off to tell him what has passed.

ACT III

Scene i   *Enter* DUKE *[disguised as a Friar] and* PROVOST
with CLAUDIO.

DUKE   So then you hope of pardon from Lord Angelo?

CLAUDIO   The miserable have no other medicine
　　　But only hope.
　　　I have hope to live, and am prepared to die.

DUKE   Be absolute for death; either death or life   5
　　　Shall thereby be the sweeter. Reason thus with life:
　　　If I do lose thee, I do lose a thing
　　　That none but fools would keep; a breath thou art,
　　　Servile° to all the skyey° influences
　　　That dost this habitation where thou keep'st   10
　　　Hourly afflict. Merely, thou art death's fool,
　　　For him thou labour'st by thy flight to shun
　　　And yet run'st toward him still. Thou art not noble,
　　　For all th'accommodations that thou bear'st
　　　Are nursed by baseness. Thou'rt by no means valiant,   15
　　　For thou dost fear the soft and tender fork°
　　　Of a poor worm. Thy best of rest is sleep,
　　　And that thou oft provok'st, yet grossly fear'st
　　　Thy death, which is no more. Thou art not thyself,
　　　For thou exists on many a thousand grains   20
　　　That issue out of dust. Happy thou art not,
　　　For what thou hast not, still thou striv'st to get,
　　　And what thou hast, forget'st. Thou art not certain,
　　　For thy complexion shifts to strange effects
　　　After the moon. If thou art rich, thou'rt poor,   25
　　　For like an ass, whose back with ingots° bows,
　　　Thou bear'st thy heavy riches but a journey,

ACT III. Scene i

1-5   The Duke enters the prison area, already talking to Claudio; the Provost is also present, but it is not clear whether or not he remains close enough to hear the conversations. He does, at least, witness the body language between prisoner and confessor and this is important as the Duke is anxious to convince him and Claudio that he really is a Friar. The Provost probably moves across to the other side of the stage, to allow a private conversation to take place, as the Duke expresses surprise that Claudio still hopes for mercy from Angelo. This declaration of hope leads the Duke into his following set-piece performance as a Friar preparing the prisoner for death.

servant to   heavenly

5-47   Throughout this next speech the Duke seems to revel in the complex game that he is playing with Claudio as he performs the role of the Friar. The Duke seems to warm to this role as he builds his argument to Claudio, convincing him that life is not so good or important and that death should be embraced. The Duke begins with a poetical and philosophical tone but ends with a passion that suggests he is speaking from the heart; it is as though by the end of the speech he has forgotten that he is playing a role and has, in effect, started to grapple with his own sentiments. By the end of this powerful speech (41), Claudio seems to have accepted the Duke's perspective and cries out for death to take him: "Let it come on" (43). However, at the very moment that Claudio says he is ready for death, the voice of Isabella is heard as she approaches the cell. This breaks the momentary spell and the Duke, unaware of who is coming, rapidly takes his leave, not wishing to be seen there by anyone. Recent research suggesting that Shakespeare may have had a Catholic education and once was in training as a priest may shed some light on the extraordinary

forked tongue, i.e., bite

bars of cast metal

And death unloads thee. Friend hast thou none,
For thine own bowels which do call thee sire,
The mere effusion° of thy proper loins,   30
Do curse the gout, serpigo,° and the rheum°
For ending thee no sooner. Thou has nor youth, nor age,
But as it were an after-dinner's sleep
Dreaming on both, for all thy blessèd youth
Becomes as agèd, and doth beg the alms   35
Of palsied-eld;° and when thou art old and rich,
Thou hast neither heat, affection, limb, nor beauty
To make thy riches pleasant. What's yet in this
That bears the name of life? Yet in this life
Lie hid more thousand deaths, yet death we fear   40
That makes these odds all even.

CLAUDIO   I humbly thank you.
To sue° to live, I find I seek to die,
And seeking death, find life. Let it come on.

ISABELLA   [*Within.*] What hoa? Peace here, grace, and good
company.   45

PROVOST   Who's there? Come in, the wish deserves a welcome.

DUKE   [*To* CLAUDIO.] Dear sir, ere long I'll visit you again.

CLAUDIO   Most holy sir, I thank you.

Enter ISABELLA.

ISABELLA   My business is a word or two with Claudio.

PROVOST   And very welcome. Look, Signior, here's your sister.   50

DUKE   Provost, a word with you.

PROVOST   As many as you please.

DUKE   Bring me to hear them speak where I may be concealed.

[*Exeunt* DUKE *and* PROVOST.]

CLAUDIO   Now sister, what's the comfort?

ISABELLA   Why,

pleasure that the Duke seems to find in his assumed role.

emission

a skin disease   rheuma-
    tism

palsied elders

plead

48-52   As the Duke is about to exit he suddenly hears that it is Claudio's sister who has arrived and on hearing this he changes his mind; he cannot resist the idea of hearing what she has to say and either playfully or clumsily, depending on interpretation of his character, asks the Provost to conceal him in the room. The Provost places the Duke in a position where his reactions can be seen by the audience and himself exits.

53-71   Although he has just declared to the Duke that he is ready for death, his conversion is short lived as Claudio immediately asks Isabella if there is

As all comforts are: most good, most good indeed.
Lord Angelo, having affairs to heaven,   55
Intends you for his swift ambassador,
Where you shall be an everlasting lieger.°
Therefore your best appointment make with speed,
Tomorrow you set on.

CLAUDIO   Is there no remedy?

ISABELLA   None, but such remedy as, to save a head,   60
To cleave a heart in twain.

CLAUDIO   But is there any?

ISABELLA   Yes, brother, you may live.
There is a devilish mercy in the judge,
If you'll implore it, that will free your life   65
But fetter you till death.

CLAUDIO   Perpetual durance°?

ISABELLA   Aye, just, perpetual durance, a restraint
Though all the world's vastidity° you had
To a determined scope.

CLAUDIO   But in what nature?

ISABELLA   In such a one as, you consenting to't,   70
Would bark° your honor from that trunk you bear,
And leave you naked.

CLAUDIO   Let me know the point.

ISABELLA   Oh, I do fear thee Claudio, and I quake,
Lest thou a feverous life shouldst entertain,
And six or seven winters more respect   75
Than a perpetual honor. Dar'st thou die?
The sense of death is most in apprehension,
And the poor beetle that we tread upon
In corporal sufferance finds a pang as great
As when a giant dies.

CLAUDIO   But why give you me this shame?   80
Think you I can a resolution fetch
From flow'ry tenderness? If I must die,
I will encounter darkness as a bride

lodger

any good news: "What's the comfort?" Isabella explains that he must prepare himself for the execution, but Claudio jumps on her unfinished half line (59) with another plea for news of any hope: "Is there no remedy?" Isabella's response is nebulous and leads Claudio anxiously to again, impatiently, finish her verse-line as he once again looks for an alternative to death: "But is there any?" (62). Again, Isabella avoids precisely explaining what has happened but alludes to a possible change of situation. Claudio, confused and desperate, believes she is referring to life imprisonment as he finishes another of her lines (66). Isabella plays with his misunderstanding of her words as she mulls over the words "perpetual durance" that she uses in a non-literal, spiritual context. The contrast between the spiritual sister and the earthbound brother is, almost humorously clear as, again, interrupting her obtuse phrasing he agitatedly demands to know what she is referring to: "But in what nature?" Once again Isabella avoids the question and Claudio explodes with impatience and probably grabs hold of her as he shouts, finishing another of her verse-lines, "Let me know the point" (72). His blunt, direct turn of phrase is in stark contrast to Isabella's heightened diction.

imprisonment

vastness

strip

73-97   Isabella changes focus and suggests that Claudio might not be honorable when faced with a choice between death and shame; she manipulates him to respond that he does not fear death and does not need comforting words. There is a short pause after Claudio's final half line (84) as Isabella feels emotion well up inside her with this profession of courage from Claudio. She now believes that he has declared that he will act honorably and she stops her caution as she begins to pour out her scorn and disgust for Angelo. At the end of her tirade, with total confidence that her brother will share the same reactions, she finally explains to Claudio, in simple language, what Angelo has proposed (97-98).

And hug it in mine arms.

ISABELLA   There spake my brother, there my father's grave   85
Did utter forth a voice! Yes, thou must die;
Thou art too noble to conserve a life
In base appliances.° This outward-sainted deputy,
Whose settled visage and deliberate word
Nips youth i'th'head, and follies doth enew°   90
As falcon doth the fowl, is yet a devil;
His filth within being cast, he would appear
A pond as deep as hell.

CLAUDIO   The prenzie° Angelo?

ISABELLA   O, 'tis the cunning livery of hell,
The damned'st body to invest and cover   95
In prenzie gards!° Dost thou think, Claudio,
If I would yield him my virginity
Thou might'st be freed?

CLAUDIO   Oh heavens, it cannot be!

ISABELLA   Yes, he would giv't thee, from this rank offense,
So to offend him still. This night's the time   100
That I should do what I abhor to name,
Or else thou diest tomorrow.

CLAUDIO   Thou shalt not do't.

ISABELLA   O, were it but my life,
I'd throw it down for your deliverance   105
As frankly as a pin.

CLAUDIO   Thanks, dear Isabel.

ISABELLA   Be ready, Claudio, for your death tomorrow.

CLAUDIO   Yes. Has he affections in him
That thus can make him bite the law by th'nose
When he would force it? Sure it is no sin,   110
Or of the deadly seven it is the least.

ISABELLA   Which is the least?

CLAUDIO   If it were damnable, he being so wise,
Why would he for the momentary trick

applications

drive into water

falsely rich

rich clothing

99-103 Isabella ends the explanation by telling Claudio that if she does not sleep with Angelo this night he, Claudio, must die tomorrow. Claudio does not respond immediately but allows a short pause after Isabella's haunting, incomplete verse-line "Or else thou diest tomorrow." Then, perhaps unconvincingly, he declares "Thou shalt not do't" (102).

108-35 Suddenly, the tone and direction of the scene changes as Claudio begins to realise the full reality of the situation and starts to suggest that losing her virginity to save her brothers life may not be such a great sin. Isabella can hardly believe what she is hearing and declares that to live in shame is worse than death. The word death, however, lingers in all Claudio's thoughts as he expresses his real fear and horror of the prospect of dying; he compares the terror of death to any kind of life and ends with a desperate plea to be allowed to live. He collapses com-

Be perdurably° fined? Oh Isabel!   115

ISABELLA   What says my brother?

CLAUDIO   Death is a fearful thing.

ISABELLA   And shamèd life, a hateful.

CLAUDIO   Aye, but to die, and go we know not where,
    To lie in cold obstruction and to rot,   120
    This sensible warm motion° to become
    A kneaded clod,° and the delighted spirit
    To bathe in fiery floods or to reside
    In thrilling region of thick-ribbèd ice,
    To be imprisoned in the viewless winds   125
    And blown with restless violence round about
    The pendant world, or to be worse than worst
    Of those that lawless and incertain thought,
    Imagine howling, 'tis too horrible.
    The weariest and most loathèd worldly life   130
    That age, ache, perjury, and imprisonment
    Can lay on nature is a paradise
    To what we fear of death.

ISABELLA   Alas, alas!

CLAUDIO Sweet sister, let me live!   135
    What sin you do to save a brother's life,
    Nature dispenses with the deed so far
    That it becomes a virtue.

ISABELLA   Oh you beast!
    Oh faithless coward! Oh dishonest wretch!
    Wilt thou be made a man out of my vice?   140
    Is't not a kind of incest to take life
    From thine own sister's shame? What should I think?
    Heaven shield my mother played my father fair,
    For such a warped slip of wilderness
    Ne'er issued from his blood. Take my defiance,   145
    Die, perish! Might but my bending down
    Reprieve thee from thy fate, it should proceed.
    I'll pray a thousand prayers for thy death,
    No word to save thee.

enduringly

pletely, emotionally and perhaps physically as he begs his sister for life: "Sweet sister, let me live" (135).

body
trodden-on lump of earth

138-55 Isabella reacts with fury and disgust at her brother's pleas as Claudio continues to tearfully beg her to listen. In performance, it is sometimes staged in a way that alienates the audience from Isabella when she seems too immovable and unrelenting toward Claudio. It is possible to interpret Isabella throughout the play as a woman out of touch with feelings and emotion and afraid of her own sexuality; it is only at the end of the play that she, perhaps, begins to learn the importance of these aspects of her nature. However, it is also possible for the Isabella to be played more sympathetically and for the audience to understand the passion of her conviction, particularly when Claudio seems cowardly and small with his tearful begging. This climactic moment is broken by the Duke's abrupt intervention (155), perhaps at a point when Isabella has turned to leave.

CLAUDIO   Nay, hear me, Isabel!   150

ISABELLA   Oh fie, fie, fie!
Thy sin's not accidental, but a trade.
Mercy to thee would prove itself a bawd,
'Tis best that thou diest quickly.

CLAUDIO   Oh hear me, Isabella!   155

[*Enter* DUKE, disguised as a Friar.]

DUKE   Vouchsafe a word, young sister, but one word.

ISABELLA   What is your will?

DUKE   Might you dispense with your leisure, I would by and by
have some speech with you. The satisfaction I would require
is likewise your own benefit.   160

ISABELLA   I have no superfluous leisure, my stay must be stolen
out of other affairs, but I will attend you awhile.

DUKE   [*Aside to* CLAUDIO.] Son, I have overheard what hath
passed between you and your sister. Angelo had never the
purpose to corrupt her; only he hath made an assay° of her   165
virtue, to practice his judgement with the disposition of
natures. She, having the truth of honor in her, hath made
him that gracious denial which he is most glad to receive. I
am confessor to Angelo, and I know this to be true; therefore
prepare yourself to death. Do not satisfy your resolution   170
with hopes that are fallible; tomorrow you must die. Go to
your knees and make ready.

CLAUDIO   Let me ask my sister pardon. I am so out of love with
life that I will sue to be rid of it.

DUKE   Hold you there. Farewell.   [*Exit* CLAUDIO.] 175
Provost, a word with you.

[*Enter* PROVOST.]

PROVOST   What's your will, Father?

DUKE   That now you are come, you will be gone. Leave me a
while with the maid, my mind promises with my habit, no

trial

156-79 As the Duke asks Isabella to wait for a moment, he speaks privately with Claudio. His simple, direct prose helps to lower the emotional temperature as he convinces Claudio that Angelo has offered the deal to Isabella only as a test of her virtue. Claudio, now calmer, accepts the explanation and, consequently, his own inevitable execution.

There is an uncertain moment between the Duke and the Provost as the Duke asks now to be left alone with Isabella; it is as though the Duke does not want him to hear the plot that he is about to reveal to Isabella. In turn, the Provost is uncertain at leaving Isabella alone with the Duke and needs to be reassured by the Duke that "my mind promises with my habit, no loss shall touch her by my company" (179). Perhaps the Provost is suspicious about this Friar who seems to be behaving oddly, first hiding to eavesdrop and then secretly speaking with both brother and sister.

loss shall touch her by my company.   180

PROVOST   In good time.   *Exit.*

DUKE   The hand that hath made you fair hath made you good.
The goodness that is cheap in beauty makes beauty brief in
goodness, but grace, being the soul of your complexion, shall
keep the body of it ever fair. The assault that Angelo hath   185
made to you, fortune hath conveyed to my understanding,
and but that frailty hath examples for his falling, I should
wonder at Angelo. How will you do to content this substitute
and to save your brother?

ISABELLA   I am now going to resolve him: I had rather my   190
brother die by the law than my son should be unlawfully
born. But, oh, how much is the good Duke deceived in
Angelo! If ever he return, and I can speak to him, I will open
my lips in vain, or discover his government.

DUKE   That shall not be much amiss. Yet, as the matter now   195
stands, he will avoid your accusation. He made trial of you
only. Therefore fasten your ear on my advisings: to the love
I have in doing good, a remedy presents itself. I do make
myself believe that you may most uprighteously do a poor
wronged lady a merited benefit, redeem your brother from   200
the angry law, do no stain to your own gracious person, and
much please the absent Duke, if peradventure he shall ever
return to have hearing of this business.

ISABELLA   Let me hear you speak farther. I have spirit to do
anything that appears not foul in the truth of my spirit.   205

DUKE   Virtue is bold, and goodness never fearful.
Have you not heard speak of Mariana, the sister of Frederick,
the great soldier who miscarried at sea?

ISABELLA   I have heard of the lady, and good words went with
her name.   210

DUKE   She should this Angelo have married, was affianced to her
oath, and the nuptial appointed; between which time of the
contract and limit of the solemnity, her brother Frederick was
wracked at sea, having in that perished vessel the dowry of
his sister. But mark how heavily this befell to the poor gentle- 215

181-230 As the Provost leaves, the Duke rapidly outlines his plan, still employing direct, concise prose. Isabella learns of the past relationship between Angelo and Mariana that was broken when her brother and the family fortune was lost at sea and Angelo promptly broke off their engagement. This new information is also interesting for the audience as it further indicates the extent of Angelo's hypocrisy whilst also shedding light on the Duke's original claim to be testing Angelo. It reminds the audience of how little they understand or believe the Duke's declared motives of leaving Angelo in command in the first place.

woman. There she lost a noble and renowned brother, in his
love toward her, ever most kind and natural; with him the
portion and sinew of her fortune, her marriage dowry; with
both, her combinate-husband,° this well-seeming° Angelo.

ISABELLA   Can this be so? Did Angelo so leave her?   220

DUKE   Left her in her tears and dried not one of them with his
comfort, swallowed his vows whole, pretending in her
discoveries of dishonor; in few,° bestowed her on her own
lamentation, which she yet wears for his sake, and he, a
marble to her tears, is washed with them but relents not.   225

ISABELLA   What a merit were it in death to take this poor maid
from the world? What corruption in this life, that it will let
this man live? But how out of this can she avail?

DUKE   It is a rupture that you may easily heal, and the cure of
it not only saves your brother but keeps you from dishonor   230
in doing it.

ISABELLA   Show me how, good Father.

DUKE   This forenamed maid hath yet in her the continuance of her
first affection; his unjust unkindness, that in all reason should
have quenched her love, hath, like an impediment in the cur-   235
rent, made it more violent and unruly. Go you to Angelo, answer his requiring with a plausible obedience, agree with his
demands to the point, only refer yourself to this advantage:
first, that your stay with him may not be long; that the time
may have all shadow and silence in it; and the place answer   240
to convenience. This being granted in course, and now follows
all: we shall advise this wronged maid to stead° up your
appointment, go in your place. If the encounter acknowledge
itself hereafter, it may compel him to her recompence, and
here by this is your brother saved, your honor untainted, the   245
poor Mariana advantaged, and the corrupt deputy scaled.°
The maid will I frame° and make fit for his attempt. If you
think well to carry this as you may, the doubleness of the benefit defends the deceit from reproof. What think you of it?

ISABELLA   The image of it gives me content already, and I trust   250
it will grow to a most prosperous perfection.

contracted husband   false

few words

keep

weighed correctly
prepare

233-59   The Duke explains the proposed bed-trick
and Isabella needs little convincing to agree. The
tone of the scene brightens as a way out for all
becomes clear. Isabella becomes excited and can
hardly contain her joy (250) as she accepts the plan.
Isabella exits from the scene as she speeds off to
move the plan forward and the Duke is left alone for
a moment on the stage, watching her leave as she
calls out farewell. It is possible for the actor to use
this moment to show his growing attraction toward
Isabella and it is possible that Isabella fuels this by
embracing him, a moment earlier, as she feels relief
at having been given a way out.

However, this clumsy and unlikely plotting
does pose some difficult questions in production:
does Mariana need to look physically like Isabella to
make it all credible and how does the instant agreement to this trick of dubious moral worth sit with the
character of the pure and incorruptible Isabella? In
some productions the thinness of the plotting is
ignored or even featured for comic effect, as in
Stephen Pimlott's production where " the improbabil-
ity of the device is emphasised by the fact that one is
blonde and the other black" (*Time Out*, 14 June
1995). In Trevor Nunn's version an attempt was
made to explain Isabella's agreement "by getting the
disguised Duke to unfurl a sheaf of press cuttings

DUKE   It lies much in your holding up. Haste you speedily to
        Angelo; if for this night he entreat you to his bed, give him
        promise of satisfaction. I will presently to Saint Luke's;
        there at the moated grange resides this dejected Mariana.   255
        At that place call upon me and dispatch with Angelo, that it
        may be quickly.

ISABELLA   I thank you for this comfort. Fare you well, good
        Father.   *Exit.*

               Enter ELBOW *and* OFFICERS *with* POMPEY.

ELBOW   Nay, if there be no remedy for it but that you will   260
        needs buy and sell men and women like beasts, we shall
        have all the world drink brown and white bastard.°

DUKE   Oh heavens, what stuff is here?

POMPEY   'Twas never merry world since of two usuries the
        merriest° was put down, and the worser° allowed by order   265
        of law; a furred gown to keep him warm, and furred with
        fox and lambskins too, to signify that craft, being richer
        than innocency, stands for the facing.°

ELBOW   Come your way, sir. 'Bless you, good Father Friar.

DUKE   And you, good brother father. What offense hath this   270
        man made you, sir?

ELBOW   Marry, sir, he hath offended the law, and, sir, we take
        him to be a thief too, sir, for we have found upon him, sir, a
        strange pick-lock,° which we have sent to the deputy.

DUKE   [*To* POMPEY.] Fie, sirrah, a bawd, a wicked bawd!   275
        The evil that thou causest to be done,
        That is thy means to live. Do thou but think
        What 'tis to cram a maw° or clothe a back
        From such a filthy vice? Say to thyself,
        'From their abominable and beastly touches   280
        I drink, I eat away myself and live.'
        Canst thou believe thy living is a life
        So stinkingly depending? Go mend, go mend.

POMPEY   Indeed, it does stink in some sort, sir, but yet, sir, I

detailing the misfortunes of the jilted Mariana" (*The Guardian*, 12 March 1992).

sweet wine, pun on "illegitimate child of mixed-race"

i.e., fornication   i.e., usury

inner edge, pun on "boasting"

259-68   This entrance can also be seen as a completely new scene, located somewhere outside or in another space entirely. It makes little difference as far as the audience is concerned as the Duke is still on stage, linking the two sections, and the precise location is rarely important in this play that is constructed around a number of central, intense and personal confrontations that have little relationship to surroundings. Either way, the themes of prisoners and justice are continued, albeit in comic form, and Elbow, Pompey and officers enter with noise and commotion as Elbow argues with Pompey about the practice of prostitution. The Duke has a bemused aside to the audience, "Oh heavens, what stuff is here?" as Pompey defends prostitution as a lesser crime than usury that goes unpunished. The tone of the play has changed radically, as it does so often in this play; the serious discussions about crime and punishment at the heart if the earlier part of Act III now give way to brash, comic musings.

lock-picking device

stuff a stomach

270-95   The Duke enters into the humorous mood of the scene and returns Elbow's twisted greeting (260) with his own version: "And you, good brother father..." (270). As Elbow explains that Pompey has been found with a "pick-lock," the Duke breaks into satiric, heightened verse that sounds like a hell-fire sermon from the pulpit. Pompey and Elbow take it at face value as the Duke tells Elbow to take Pompey of to prison. Elbow reintroduces to the play the theme of justice, particularly in relationship to the deeds of Angelo. The Duke momentarily becomes serious and reflective as he creates a rhyming couplet on the subject of innocence and hypocrisy (294-295). The couplet is probably shared directly with the audience rather than with the characters on stage as Lucio joins the group; the Duke is observing the comings and goings on stage throughout this sequence and his comments are not heard by others on stage.

would prove—   285

DUKE   Nay, if the devil have given thee proofs for sin,
        Thou wilt prove his. Take him to prison, Officer.
        Correction and instruction must both work
        Ere this rude beast will profit.

ELBOW   He must before the deputy, sir, he has given him warn- 290
        ing: the deputy cannot abide a whore-master. If he be a
        whore-monger and comes before him, he were as good go a
        mile on his errand.

DUKE   That we were all, as some would seem to be,
        From our faults, as faults from seeming, free.   295

                        Enter LUCIO.

ELBOW   His neck will come to your waist, a cord,° sir.

POMPEY I spy comfort, I cry bail. Here's a gentleman, and a
        friend of mine.

LUCIO   How now, noble Pompey? What, at the wheels of
        Caesar? Art thou led in triumph? What, is there none of 300
        Pygmalion's° images° newly made woman to be had now
        for putting the hand in the pocket and extracting clutched?
        What reply? Ha? What sayest thou to this tune, matter, and
        method? Is't not drowned i'th' last rain? Ha? What sayest
        thou, trot?° Is the world as it was, man? Which is the way? 305
        Is it sad, and few words? Or how? The trick of it?

DUKE   Still thus, and thus; still worse!

LUCIO   How doth my dear morsel, thy mistress? Procures° she
        still? Ha?

POMPEY 'Troth, sir, she hath eaten up all her beef,° and she is 310
        herself in the tub.°

LUCIO   Why 'tis good. It is the right of it, it must be so. Ever
        your fresh whore and your powdered bawd, an unshunned°
        consequence, it must be so. Art going to prison, Pompey?

POMPEY Yes, 'faith, sir.   315

LUCIO   Why 'tis not amiss Pompey, farewell. Go say I sent thee

289-317 Instead of helping him with his bail, as anticipated by Pompey (288), Lucio teases him mercilessly and actually relishes the prospect of Elbow taking Pompey off to prison. Pompey is genuinely surprised that his "friend" so easily betrays his trust. During the cruel teasing that follows, as Lucio runs about on stage clowning in mock admiration of the "noble Pompey" (289), Lucio demonstrates his cold, mean character, whereas Pompey's pathetic and simple manner gains some sympathy, in spite of his crimes.

belt, puns on "noose"

mythical creator's   statues,
    pun on "prostitutes"

hag

pimps

i.e. medicine

i.e. taking the cure for venereal
    disease

inevitable

thither. For debt, Pompey? Or how?

ELBOW   For being a bawd, for being a bawd.

LUCIO   Well, then, imprison him. If imprisonment be the due of
a bawd, why 'tis his right. Bawd is he doubtless, and of   320
antiquity too, bawd-born.° Farewell, good Pompey. Com-
mend me to the prison, Pompey; you will turn good husband now, Pompey, you will keep the house.

POMPEY   I hope, sir, your good worship will be my bail?

LUCIO   No, indeed, will I not, Pompey, it is not the wear.° I   325
will pray, Pompey, to increase your bondage if you take it
not patiently. Why, your mettle is the more. Adieu, trusty
Pompey. Bless you, Friar.

DUKE   And you.

LUCIO   Does Bridget paint° still, Pompey? Ha?   330

ELBOW   [*To* POMPEY.] Come your ways, sir, come.

POMPEY   You will not bail me then, sir?

LUCIO   Then Pompey, nor now. What news abroad, Friar? What
news?

ELBOW   Come your ways, sir, come.   335

LUCIO   Go to kennel, Pompey, go.

                    [*Exeunt* ELBOW *and* OFFICERS *with* POMPEY.]
What news, Friar, of the Duke?

DUKE   I know none. Can you tell me of any?

LUCIO   Some say he is with the Emperor of Russia; other some,
he is in Rome. But where is he, think you?   340

DUKE   I know not where, but wheresoever I wish him well.

LUCIO   It was a mad, fantastical° trick of him to steal from the
state and usurp the beggary he was never born to. Lord
Angelo dukes it well in his absence, he puts transgression to't.

DUKE   He does well in't.   345

LUCIO   A little more lenity to lechery would do no harm in him.

born of a bawd; born to be a
    bawd

fashion

apply heavy makeup

336-58 Elbow, Pompey and the officers exit, leaving Lucio and the Duke alone on stage. After trying
for a few moments to change the tone of his language, and speak with the man he believes to be a
friar in an appropriate way, Lucio soon reverts to his
high humour and vicious tongue as he scorns
Angelo: "when he makes water, his urine is congealed ice" (357). However, he also expresses to the
Duke the general public response to Angelo's new
regime and his criticism is armed with sharp wit.

impulsive

Something too crabbed° that way, Friar.

DUKE   It is too general a vice, and severity must cure it.

LUCIO   Yes, in good sooth, the vice is of a great kindred; it is
well allied, but it is impossible to extirp° it quite, Friar,   350
till eating and drinking be put down. They say this Angelo
was not made° by man and woman after this downright
way of creation. Is it true, think you?

DUKE   How should he be made then?

LUCIO   Some report, a sea-maid° spawned him; some, that he   355
was begot between two stock-fishes.° But it is certain that
when he makes water, his urine is congealed ice, that I know
to be true, and he is a motion generative,° that's infallible.

DUKE   You are pleasant, sir, and speak apace.

LUCIO   Why, what a ruthless thing is this in him, for the   360
rebellion of a codpiece,° to take away the life of a man?
Would the Duke that is absent have done this? Ere he would
have hanged a man for the getting a hundred bastards, he
would have paid for the nursing a thousand. He had some
feeling of the sport, he knew the service, and that instructed 365
him to mercy.

DUKE   I never heard the absent Duke much detected for women,
he was not inclined that way.

LUCIO   Oh, sir, you are deceived.

DUKE   'Tis not possible.   370

LUCIO   Who, not the Duke? Yes, your beggar of fifty, and his use
was to put a ducket in her clack-dish.° The Duke had crochets°
in him. He would be drunk too, that let me inform you.

DUKE   You do him wrong, surely.

LUCIO   Sir, I was an inward° of his. A shy fellow was the Duke,   375
and I believe I know the cause of his withdrawing.

DUKE   What, I prithee, might be the cause?

LUCIO   No, pardon; 'tis a secret must be locked within the teeth
and the lips. But this I can let you understand, the greater

disagreeable

root up

conceived

mermaid
dried fish

sexless puppet

i.e., male genitals

360-67   Any amusement the Duke might have had at Lucio's vitriolic attack on Angelo soon gives way to surprise as Lucio turns his tongue toward the Duke himself. Lucio compares the Duke and Angelo but begins to suggest that the Duke would have been more lenient with adulterers and prostitutes because he himself "had some feeling for the sport" (364). The Duke tries to contain his irritation as he fights to stay in character as the Friar while defending himself; there is humor within the comic tension as he tries to appear outwardly calm and maintain an elegant and distant turn of phrase (367).

coin in her beggar's dish, i.e.,
    fornicate   perverse
    whims

confidant

371-82   Lucio expands on his description of the Duke by implying that he has sexual motives when he gives to charity and is a drunkard. The Duke is so stunned by the growing list of insults that he can hardly utter responses, and he struggles to defend himself. Lucio, now unstoppable in his flow, begins to explain that the Duke is in addition, "A very superficial, ignorant, unweighing fellow." (382).

file of the subject held the Duke to be wise.   380

DUKE   Wise? Why no question but he was.

LUCIO   A very superficial, ignorant, unweighing fellow.

DUKE   Either this is envy in you, folly, or mistaking. The very
        stream of his life and the business he hath helmed must
        upon a warranted need give him a better proclamation. Let   385
        him be but testimonied in his own bringings forth, and he
        shall appear to the envious a scholar, a statesman, and a
        soldier. Therefore you speak unskilfully, or, if your
        knowledge be more, it is much darkened in your malice.

LUCIO   Sir, I know him, and I love him.   390

DUKE   Love talks with better knowledge, and knowledge with
        dearer love.

LUCIO   Come, sir, I know what I know.

DUKE   I can hardly believe that, since you know not what you
        speak. But if ever the Duke return, as our prayers are he   395
        may, let me desire you to make your answer before him. If
        it be honest you have spoke, you have courage to maintain
        it. I am bound to call upon you, and I pray you, your name?

LUCIO   Sir, my name is Lucio, well known to the Duke.

DUKE   He shall know you better, sir, if I may live to report you. 400

LUCIO   I fear you not.

DUKE   Oh, you hope the Duke will return no more, or you
        imagine me too unhurtful an opposite, but indeed I can do
        you little harm. You'll forswear this again?

LUCIO   I'll be hanged first. Thou art deceived in me, Friar. But   405
        no more of this. Canst thou tell if Claudio die tomorrow, or
        no?

DUKE   Why should he die, sir?

LUCIO   Why? For filling a bottle with a tundish.° I would the
        Duke we talk of were returned again; this ungenitured agent° 410
        will un-people the province with continency.° Sparrows must
        not build in his house-eaves, because they are lecherous. The

383-404 At this point, the Duke can contain his irritation no longer and bursts out with a full defense of his own character. Lucio, however, is unimpressed and sticks to his guns: "Come, sir, I know what I know." (393). At this point, the tone of the Duke changes, and he loses patience with Lucio; now he begins to threaten him and dare him to repeat his words when the Duke returns. Lucio is unabashed and maintains his bravado as the Duke, in anger, almost forgets that he is still in disguise as the Friar. He recovers his control as he remembers the role he is playing: "but indeed I can do you little harm" (403). Throughout this sequence the audience is encouraged to laugh at the Duke as he is provoked by Lucio and the insults heaped upon him; the Duke's stature is damaged in this exchange whereas Lucio emerges from the scene unscathed.

funnel, with bawdy meaning
sexless substitute
celibacy

405-24 After this moment of tension, Lucio changes the subject back to the fate of Claudio. He again expresses his hatred of Angelo and concludes that in spite of everything he would like to see the Duke return. With dubious praise for the Duke, in comparison with Angelo, he exits leaving the Duke alone for a moment on stage. In his short soliloquy the Duke meditates on how even great and powerful men cannot escape slander and malice. This is an important moment for his character as the trappings of his role as the Duke have been stripped bare and he remembers that he is indeed only human and has many limits to his power.

Duke yet would have dark deeds darkly answered, he would
never bring them to light. Would he were returned! Marry,
this Claudio is condemned for untrussing.° Farewell, good   415
Friar, I prithee pray for me. The Duke, I say to thee again,
would eat mutton° on Fridays.° He's now past it, yet, and I
say to thee, he would mouth° with a beggar though she smelt°
brown bread and garlic. Say that I said so. Farewell.   *Exit.*

DUKE   No might nor greatness in mortality   420
Can censure 'scape°; back-wounding calumny
The whitest virtue strikes. What king so strong
Can tie the gall up in the slanderous tongue?
But who comes here?

Enter ESCALUS, PROVOST, [*and* OFFICERS *with*] MISTRESS OVERDONE.

ESCALUS   Go, away with her to prison.   425

MISTRESS OVERDONE   Good my lord, be good to me, your honor is
accounted a merciful man. Good my lord!

ESCALUS   Double and treble admonition and still forfeit in the
same kind? This would make mercy swear and play the tyrant.

PROVOST A bawd of eleven years continuance, may it please   430
your honor.

MISTRESS OVERDONE   My lord, this is one Lucio's information
against me. Mistress Kate Keepdown was with child by him
in the Duke's time, he promised her marriage. His child is a
year and a quarter old come Phillip and Jacob.° I have kept   435
it myself, and see how he goes about to abuse me.

ESCALUS   That fellow is a fellow of much license. Let him be
called before us. Away with her to prison. Go to, no more
words.   [*Exeunt* OFFICERS *with* MISTRESS OVERDONE.]
Provost, my brother Angelo will not be altered, Claudio   440
must die tomorrow. Let him be furnished with divines and
have all charitable preparation. If my brother wrought by
my pity, it should not be so with him.

PROVOST   So please you, this friar hath been with him and
advised him for th'entertainment of death.   445

undressing

lamb, puns on "use a whore"
   i.e., fastdays

kiss   smelled of

escape

424-38   The moment of quietness is broken by the loud arrival of Escalus, the Provost and Mistress Overdone as prisoner. She is struggling and shouting her innocence as they escort her to prison. We hear further condemnation of Lucio as she complains that it is he, a criminal who has fathered a child with a mistress, who has informed on her. There is little sympathy for her from Escalus and the Provost as she is led away to prison. There is, perhaps, a smile from the Duke as Escalus calls for Lucio to be arrested (437). Mistress Overdone is clearly still struggling and complaining strenuously with improvised protestations as she is dragged off the stage: "Go to, no more words" (438).

i.e., their feast-day, May 1

444-53   The rhythm and tone of the scene changes again as Escalus and the Provost discuss Claudio's execution for the following morning. Escalus is keen to let the Provost know that he has tried to change

ESCALUS   Good even°, good Father.

DUKE   Bliss and goodness on you.

ESCALUS   Of whence are you?

DUKE   Not of this country, though my chance is now
    To use it for my time. I am a brother   450
    Of gracious order, late come from the See°
    In special business from his Holiness.

ESCALUS   What news abroad i'th world?

DUKE   None, but that there is so great a fever on goodness that
    the dissolution of it must cure it. Novelty is only in request,   455
    and as it is as dangerous to be aged in any kind of course as
    it is virtuous to be constant in any undertaking. There is
    scarce truth enough alive to make societies secure, but
    security enough to make fellowships accurst. Much upon
    this riddle runs the wisdom of the world. This news is old   460
    enough, yet it is everyday's news. I pray you, sir, of what
    disposition was the Duke?

ESCALUS   One that, above all other strifes, contended especially
    to know himself.

DUKE   What pleasure was he given to?   465

ESCALUS   Rather rejoicing to see another merry than merry at
    anything which professed to make him rejoice. A gentleman
    of all temperance. But leave we him to his events, with a
    prayer they may prove prosperous, and let me desire to
    know how you find Claudio prepared. I am made to under-   470
    stand that you have lent him visitation.

DUKE   He professes to have received no sinister measure from
    his judge, but most willingly humbles himself to the
    determination of justice. Yet had he framed to himself, by
    the instruction of his frailty, many deceiving promises of   475
    life, which I, by my good leisure, have discredited to him,
    and now is he resolved to die.

ESCALUS   You have paid the heavens your function, and the
    prisoner the very debt of your calling. I have labored for the
    poor gentleman, to the extremest shore of my modesty, but   480

evening

Angelo's mind. At this point the Duke, who has until now been some distance from the others, steps forward and is introduced by the Provost to Escalus (446). The credibility of the Duke's disguise is tested here, as Escalus speaks with him for the first time; unlike the cases of Lucio and the Provost, the audience knows Escalus has known the Duke for a long time.

papal seat

454-86 After giving a brief negative reflection on the world in general (454-462), the Duke, still smarting from Lucio's character assassination, asks Escalus his view of the Duke. After painting a brief sympathetic picture of a man "of all temperance" (468), Escalus returns to the theme of Claudio that is weighing heavily on his mind. After being a little comforted by the Duke's account of his meeting with Claudio, Escalus again feels the need to tell someone, this time the Duke, how hard he has tried to plead to Angelo for mercy for Claudio. Escalus is genuinely very distressed that Angelo has not listened and that Claudio must die. Escalus and the Provost exit to visit Claudio and the Duke is once again left alone to share his thoughts with the audience.

my brother-justice have I found so severe that he hath forced
me to tell him he is indeed justice.

DUKE   If his own life answer the straightness of his proceeding,
it shall become him well, wherein if he chance to fail he hath
sentenced himself.   485

ESCALUS   I am going to visit the prisoner. Fare you well.
                              [*Exeunt* ESCALUS *and* PROVOST.]

DUKE   Peace be with you.
He who the sword of heaven will bear
Should be as holy, as severe;
Pattern in himself to know,   490
Grace to stand, and virtue go;
More nor less to others paying,
Than by self-offenses weighing.
Shame to him, whose cruel striking
Kills for faults of his own liking;   495
Twice treble shame on Angelo,
To weed my vice and let his grow.
O, what may man within him hide,
Though angel on the outward side?
How may likeness made in crimes,   500
Making practice on the times,
To draw with idle spiders strings
Most ponderous and substantial things?
Craft against vice, I must apply.
With Angelo tonight shall lie   505
His old betrothèd, but despised;
So disguise shall by the disguised
Pay with falsehood, false exacting,
And perform an old contracting.   *Exit.*

487-509 The Duke soliloquizes using a series of rhyming couplets that give a heightened, philosophical impact to his thoughts as he meditates on the nature of men in relation to justice. In many ways this speech lies at the centre of the play's themes of balance, of measure for measure. The speech is constructed of a sequence of antithetical statements that show the Duke desperately trying to come to terms with a world of hypocrisy and false appearances; it is as though he is grappling with his own past attitudes to his role as supreme justice in the land and his own past failings. In focusing on Angelo's hypocrisy he is beginning to understand more about himself. The conclusion that his plan "craft" must be used to balance the "vice" of Angelo (504) is the culmination of the measure for measure theme of the speech. With a final rhyming couplet expressing a decisive conclusion he exits to prepare his plot.

ACT IV

Scene i   *Enter* Mariana *and a* Boy.

Boy   [*Sings.*] Take, oh take those lips away,
                            that so sweetly were forsworn,
                    And those eyes: the break of day,
                            lights that do mislead the morn;
                    But my kisses bring again, bring again,   5
                    Seals of love, but sealed in vain, sealed in vain.

Enter Duke [*disguised as a friar.*]

Mariana   Break off thy song and haste thee quick away,
        Here comes a man of comfort, whose advice
        Hath often stilled my brawling discontent.   [*Exit* Boy.]
        I cry you mercy, sir, and well could wish   10
        You had not found me here so musical.
        Let me excuse me, and believe me so,
        My mirth it much displeased, but pleased my woe.

Duke   'Tis good, though music oft hath such a charm
        To make bad, good, and good provoke to harm.   15
        I pray you tell me, hath anybody inquired for me here today?
        Much upon this time have I promised here to meet.

Mariana   You have not been inquired after; I have sat here all
        day.

Enter Isabella.

Duke   I do constantly believe you; the time is come even now. I   20
        shall crave your forbearance a little; maybe I will call upon
        you anon° for some advantage to yourself.

ACT IV. Scene i

1-23   This Act opens with a new tone, rhythm and setting. The music is used to take us into a more feminine world, momentarily away from the prison, the palace and the bustling streets of Vienna. The scene is probably set inside a room in the city, probably in Mariana's home—"the moated grange" at "St Luke's"—mentioned in III.i.254-255. Perhaps the decor also expresses this gentler world.

Although there has been extensive academic debate about the origin of the song and whether or not it was added to the play by another playwright at a later date, in fact it is appropriate and carefully located at this point in the play. The boy's singing and the quiet presence of Mariana transports the audience toward the human reality of a society in which there are victims; for a brief moment we leave behind the world of politics and bawdy comedy. In some productions the song is sung by Mariana herself. The song itself tells of the sadness of forsaken love as Mariana meditates on her present state since Angelo has deserted her.

As Mariana sees the Duke enter the room she stops the song, sends the boy away and steps forward, perhaps tearfully, to greet the Duke (10). It is possible that the Duke has actually been there from the beginning of the scene, silently watching Mariana and listening to the song. His reference to the music, "'Tis good" (14), may be specific rather than simply polite. He is caught up in the slow, gentle rhythm of the scene and takes a moment to muse on another paradox, or measure for measure, as the mood of the music makes him think how it can "make bad, good, and good provoke to harm" (15).

The Duke then changes the mood as he gets down to business asking if anyone has come looking for him, presumably anxiously wondering if Isabella has yet come and if his plan is on course. A moment later she arrives and Mariana is asked to exit in order to leave the Duke alone with Isabella.

presently

MARIANA   I am always bound to you.   *Exit.*

DUKE   Very well met and welcome.
  What is the news from this good deputy?   25

ISABELLA   He hath a garden circummured with brick,
  Whose western side is with a vineyard backed,
  And to that vineyard is a planchèd° gate
  That makes his opening with this bigger key.
  This other doth command a little door   30
  Which from the vineyard to the garden leads.
  There have I made my promise, upon the heavy
  Middle of the night, to call upon him.

DUKE   But shall you on your knowledge find this way?

ISABELLA   I have ta'en a due and wary note upon't.   35
  With whispering and most guilty diligence,
  In action all of precept, he did show me
  The way twice o'er.

DUKE   Are there no other tokens
  Between you 'greed° concerning her observance?

ISABELLA   No, none but only a repair i'th' dark,   40
  And that I have possessed him my most stay
  Can be but brief, for I have made him know
  I have a servant comes with me along
  That stays upon me, whose persuasion is
  I come about my brother.

DUKE   'Tis well borne up.   45
  I have not yet made known to Mariana
  A word of this. What hoa, within; come forth.

Enter MARIANA.

  I pray you be acquainted with this maid,
  She comes to do you good.

ISABELLA   I do desire the like.

DUKE   [*To* MARIANA.] Do you persuade yourself that I respect you? 50

MARIANA   Good Friar, I know you do, and have found it.

Mariana may well be puzzled by what is going on as she withdraws.

wooden

26-45 The rhythm of the scene speeds up as Isabella and the Duke discuss the details of the plot. Isabella has carried out her preparations with diligence and betrays in her tone that she is in fact enjoying the whole masquerade as she expresses her amusement at Angelo, in his enthusiasm, showing her the way in to his chambers twice (38). Similarly, she is pleased with the way she invented a waiting servant to explain the briefness that the nighttime visit to Angelo will entail. The Duke, too, seems to take pleasure and excitedly finishes her unfinished verse-line by congratulating her for her clever work: "'Tis well borne up" (45). The two characters seem to be finding a natural understanding and are being brought together by a shared feeling about all that is happening; this helps in building credibility for the Duke's proposal at the end of the play (V.i.486).

agreed

47-62 The Duke's excitement continues to grow as he loudly calls out for Mariana and then he rapidly sends them off to discuss the plan. The sense of night approaching is emphasized (55) as the plot moves forward to its coming climax.

The Duke is left alone again to soliloquize. The speech seems designed to give Isabella time to explain all to Mariana, but it seems too short for the job; perhaps, though the audience has been already drawn too far inside the story to even notice. The content of the speech is also strange and seems to be a reflection on the problems faced by rulers, surrounded by rumors and deceit. In the staging, the Duke is in the foreground as Isabella and Mariana

DUKE   Take then this your companion by the hand,
    Who hath a story ready for your ear.
    I shall attend your leisure, but make haste,
    The vaporous night approaches.   55

MARIANA   [*To* ISABELLA.] Wil't please you walk aside?
                        [MARIANA *and* ISABELLA *withdraw.*]

DUKE   O place and greatness, millions of false eyes
    Are stuck upon thee; volumes of report
    Run with these false and most contrarious quests
    Upon thy doings; thousand escapes of wit   60
    Make thee the father of their idle dream
    And rack° thee in their fancies.
                 [MARIANA *and* ISABELLA *come forward.*]
    Welcome, how agreed?

ISABELLA   She'll take the enterprise upon her, Father,
    If you advise it.

DUKE   It is not my consent,   65
    But my entreaty too.

ISABELLA   [*To* MARIANA.] Little have you to say
    When you depart from him, but soft and low,
    `Remember now my brother.'

MARIANA   Fear me not.

DUKE   Nor, gentle daughter, fear you not at all.   70
    He is your husband on a pre-contract;
    To bring you thus together, 'tis no sin,
    Sith° that the justice of your title to him
    Doth flourish the deceit. Come, let us go,
    Our corn's to reap, for yet our tithe's to sow.   *Exeunt.* 75

Scene ii   *Enter* PROVOST *and* POMPEY.

PROVOST   Come hither, sirrah. Can you cut off a man's head?

walk around in the background, deep in conversation. The effect, helped on the modern stage by lighting, should be of time telescoped, rather than a naturalistic sense of real time.

distort

63-74   The rhythm picks up again as the scene rushes to a quick end in a flurry of shared verse lines, climaxing with an upward inflected final rhyming couplet as they sweep off stage. In order to make more believable Isabella's agreement to the bed-trick idea it is a good idea to show an understanding and close connection between Mariana and her as they reenter; if Isabella feels strongly for Mariana and her suffering the audience questions less motives for agreeing to the plan. Perhaps they enter holding hands or in an embrace.

since

Scene ii

1-15   The setting moves back to the prison as the time moves toward midnight. The mood is one of

POMPEY   If the man be a bachelor, sir, I can, but if he be a
married man, he's his wife's head, and I can never cut off a
woman's head.

PROVOST   Come, sir, leave your snatches° and yield me a direct   5
answer. Tomorrow morning are to die Claudio and Barnadine. Here is in our prison a common executioner, who in his
office lacks a helper. If you will take it on you to assist him,
it shall redeem you from your gyves°; if not, you shall have
our full time of imprisonment, and your deliverance with an   10
unpitied whipping, for you have been a notorious bawd.

POMPEY   Sir, I have been an unlawful bawd, time out of mind,
but yet I will be content to be a lawful hangman. I would be
glad to receive some instruction from my fellow partner.

PROVOST   What hoa, Abhorson,° where's Abhorson there?   15

Enter ABHORSON.

ABHORSON   Do you call, sir?

PROVOST   Sirrah, here's a fellow will help you tomorrow in your
execution. If you think it meet, compound with him by the
year, and let him abide here with you; if not, use him for the
present and dismiss him. He cannot plead his estimation°   20
with you, he hath been a bawd.

ABHORSON   A bawd, sir? Fie upon him, he will discredit our
mystery.°

PROVOST   Go too, sir, you weigh equally, a feather will turn the
scale.   *Exit.*   25

POMPEY   Pray, sir, by your good favor, for surely, sir, a good
favor you have but that you have a hanging look. Do you
call, sir, your occupation a mystery?

ABHORSON   Aye, sir, a mystery.

POMPEY   Painting,° sir, I have heard say, is a mystery, and your   30
whores, sir, being members of my occupation, using painting,
do prove my occupation a mystery. But what mystery there
should be in hanging, if I should be hanged, I cannot imagine.

quibbles

black humor as the Provost employs Pompey to assist with the execution of Claudio, who readily accepts the commission in exchange for a softer sentence. The Provost, clearly unhappy about the executions set for the following day, is curt and humorless as they discuss the matter. There is more dark humor in the scene when the executioner, Abhorson, is called for (15), and the play on words in his name with "whore" and "abhor' strikes an odd and comic note.

shackles

puns on "son of a whore" and
    "abhorred one"

superior reputation

secret rite

22-40   There is a continuation of this mood as the executioner and the bawd compare professions and make value judgments about the two unpleasant trades. This sequence is typical of the black humor at work so often in the play as the plot itself stops for a few moments.

applying heavy makeup

ABHORSON   Sir, it is a mystery.

POMPEY   Proof.   35

ABHORSON   Every true man's apparel fits your thief.

POMPEY   If it be too little for your thief, your true man thinks
it big enough. If it be too big for your thief, your thief
thinks it little enough, so every true man's apparel fits your
thief.   40

Enter PROVOST.

PROVOST   Are you agreed?

POMPEY   Sir, I will serve him, for I do find your hangman is a
more penitent trade than your bawd; he doth oftener ask
forgiveness.

PROVOST   [*To* ABHORSON.] You, sirrah, provide your block and   45
your ax tomorrow, four o'clock.

ABHORSON [*To* POMPEY.] Come on, bawd, I will instruct thee in my
trade. Follow.

POMPEY   I do desire to learn, sir, and I hope, if you have
occasion to use me for your own turn, you shall find me   50
yare.° For truly, sir, for your kindness, I owe you a good turn.

PROVOST   Call hither Barnadine and Claudio.
                              [*Exeunt* ABHORSON *and* POMPEY.]
Th'one has my pity, not a jot the other,
Being a murderer, though he were my brother.

Enter CLAUDIO.

Look, here's the warrant, Claudio, for thy death.   55
'Tis now dead midnight, and by eight tomorrow
Thou must be made immortal. Where's Barnadine?

CLAUDIO   As fast locked up on sleep as guiltless labour
When it lies starkly in the traveler's bones.
He will not wake.

PROVOST   Who can do good on him?   60

41-54   The Provost reenters (40) and, still upset by what is happening, abruptly asks Abhorson to prepare his "block" and "ax" for tomorrow (45). As they prepare to exit, there is a final comic twist to the sequence as Abhorson offers to teach his trade to Pompey and Pompey, still in good humour, offers to use his trade to please Abhorson (51).

The Provost, unamused, has a brief moment alone in which he shares with the audience his lack of pity for Barnadine, who is to be executed for murder, and his compassion for Claudio (53 and 54). This quick, rhyming couplet, following a scene of black humor, allows a moment of reflection. The connection with the audience is indicative of the changing tones and rhythms of this complex play; so often humor gives way to pain and a rapidly forward-moving scene stops as a character philosophizes and deliberates about the ways of the world.

ready

55-68   Claudio enters and the Provost, uncomfortable with his task, confirms quickly to him that he must die in the morning. Claudio seems to show no emotion, as though he has at last accepted his fate. A loud knocking is heard, shattering the nighttime quietness in the prison, and the reference to "midnight" reminds us of the other action offstage concerning Isabella and Angelo.

As Claudio silently returns to his cell (62), the Provost excitedly hopes that it is a last minute reprieve for Claudio. The tension is high as the Duke

Well, go, prepare yourself.   [*Knocking within.*]
But hark, what noise?
Heaven give your spirits comfort!   [*Exit* CLAUDIO.]
                     By and by!
I hope it is some pardon or reprieve
For the most gentle Claudio.

        [*Enter* DUKE, *disguised as a Friar.*]

             Welcome Father.   65

DUKE   The best and wholesom'st spirits of the night
    Envelop you, good Provost. Who called here of late?

PROVOST   None since the curfew rung.

DUKE   Not Isabel?

PROVOST   No.   70

DUKE   They will then ere't be long.

PROVOST   What comfort is for Claudio?

DUKE   There's some in hope.

PROVOST   It is a bitter deputy.

DUKE   Not so, not so, his life is paralleled   75
    Even with the stroke and line of his great justice.
    He doth with holy abstinence subdue
    That in himself which he spurs on his power
    To qualify in others. Were he mealed° with that
    Which he corrects, then were he tyrannous,   80
    But this being so, he's just. [*Knocking within.*] Now are they
      come.   [*Exit* PROVOST.]
    This is a gentle Provost; seldom-when°
    The steelèd jailer is the friend of men.

      [*Enter* PROVOST. *Knocking within.*]

How now? What noise? That spirit's possessed with haste
That wounds th'unsisting postern° with these strokes.   85

PROVOST   There he must stay until the officer

enters and immediately moves forward the plot as he asks if anyone has yet come (67). The verse-line, rapidly shared back and forth between the Duke and the Provost (68), indicates the sudden speeding-up of the rhythm amid the increasing tension as the Duke anxiously awaits the outcome of the plan.

70-91   The Provost openly expresses his dismay at Angelo's decision to execute Claudio, "It is a bitter deputy" (74), and the Duke feigns a defense for him, while already hinting at the hypocrisy that will soon become apparent. The Duke seems to be testing the reactions of the Provost in the same way that he tests those of Angelo, Isabella, and Claudio; he is always watching intently the characters that he pushes to extremes in order to find out their true characters and feelings.

A loud knocking is again heard, again adding tension to the scene. The Provost may exit at this point to investigate and also leave the Duke alone for his aside about the Provost, but it is also possible for this aside to be staged without an actual and unnecessary exit; it is simply a question of stage positions and it is easy to organize for the Duke to be downstage of the Provost and, consequently, closer to an audience.The Provost indicates later (86) that an officer will open the door, rather than he himself. The Duke continues refusing to explain that Claudio will be reprieved but mysteriously prolongs the game and hints at a change of decision: "You shall hear more ere morning" (91).

stained

seldom is it when

unlocked back door

Arise to let him in; he is called up.

DUKE   Have you no countermand° for Claudio yet
But he must die tomorrow?

PROVOST   None, sir, none.

DUKE   As near the dawning, Provost, as it is,   90
You shall hear more ere morning.

PROVOST   Happily,
You something know, yet I believe there comes
No countermand; no such example have we.
Besides, upon the very siege of justice,
Lord Angelo hath to the public ear   95
Professed the contrary.

Enter a MESSENGER.

This is his lord's man.

DUKE   And here comes Claudio's pardon.

MESSENGER   [*Giving* PROVOST *a letter.*] My lord hath sent you this
note, and by me this further charge: that you swerve not from
the smallest article of it, neither in time, matter, or other   100
circumstance. Good morrow, for as I take it, it is almost day.

PROVOST   I shall obey him.   [*Exit* MESSENGER.]

DUKE   [*Aside.*]   This is his pardon purchased by such sin
For which the pardoner himself is in.
Hence hath offense his quick celerity
When it is borne in high authority.   105
When vice makes mercy, mercy's so extended
That for the fault's love is th'offender friended.
[*To* PROVOST.] Now, sir, what news?

PROVOST   I told you, Lord Angelo, belike, thinking me remiss
in mine office, awakens me with this unwonted putting on,   110
methinks strangely, for he hath not used it before.

DUKE   Pray you let's hear.

PROVOST   [*Reading.*] `Whatsoever you may hear to the contrary,
let Claudio be executed by four of the clock, and, in the

contrary command

97-107 The Duke cannot contain his anticipation and excitement as he leaps on the Provost's unfinished verse line (97) and finishes it as the messenger enters: "This is his lord's man". The Duke is relieved to see that it is Angelo's servant, as does the Provost, and assumes that he has come to announce the pardon. The messenger delivers a strange and precise message from Angelo that commands the Provost to do exactly what has been set down in the "note." As the Provost begins to unwrap the document and the messenger exits in the background the Duke again has a private exchange with the audience. He muses in rhyming couplets about how quickly Angelo can find mercy for a sinner when he himself indulges in the same sin.

109-119 The Provost expresses irritation that Angelo seems not to fully trust that he will do his duty, as indicated in the command delivered by the messenger from Angelo (98-101), and he then reads the document out aloud. There is a stunned silence on the stage as Angelo's proclamation is read. After the building of expectation of a reprieve, the impact of the brutal command is intense.

afternoon, Barnardine. For my better satisfaction, let me   115
have Claudio's head sent me by five. Let this be duly performed with a thought that more depends on it then we
must yet deliver. Thus fail not to do your office, as you will
answer it at your peril.' What say you to this, sir?

DUKE   What is that Barnardine who is to be executed in   120
th'afternoon?

PROVOST   A Bohemian born, but here nursed up and bred;
one that is a prisoner nine years old.

DUKE   How came it that the absent Duke had not either delivered him to his liberty or executed him? I have heard it   125
was ever his manner to do so.

PROVOST   His friends still wrought reprieves for him, and indeed
his fact till now in the government of Lord Angelo came not
to an undoubtful° proof.

DUKE   Is it now apparent?   130

PROVOST   Most manifest and not denied by himself.

DUKE   Hath he borne himself penitently in prison? How seems he
to be touched?

PROVOST   A man that apprehends death no more dreadfully but
as a drunken sleep, careless, reckless, and fearless of what's   135
past, present, or to come, insensible of mortality, and
desperately mortal.

DUKE   He wants advice.°

PROVOST   He will hear none, he hath evermore had the liberty of
the prison; give him leave to escape hence, he would not.   140
Drunk many times a day, if not many days entirely drunk.
We have very oft awaked him, as if to carry him to execution,
and showed him a seeming warrant for it, it hath not moved
him at all.

DUKE   More of him anon. There is written in your brow, Provost,   145
honesty and constancy; if I read it not truly, my ancient skill
beguiles me. But in the boldness of my cunning, I will lay
myself in hazard. Claudio, whom here you have warrant to
execute, is no greater forfeit to the law than Angelo who

120-44 The Duke's thoughts work rapidly as he formulates a new plan as his existing one begins to collapse. By ensuring from his conversation with the Provost that Barnadine is an irredeemable, drunken murderer, the Duke is able to proceed with his plan with a clear conscience and is able to recoup some of his lost credibility, although he is beginning to look increasingly less in control of the situation.

certain

needs spiritual counsel

145-169 The Duke explains to the Provost his improvised plan of substituting Barnadine's head for Claudio's, but the honest and distressed Provost refuses as he is bound by his "oath" (169). The Duke seems to enjoy working out the details of his new scheme as he demolishes each practical objection

hath sentenced him. To make you understand this in a mani- 150
fested effect, I crave but four days respite, for the which you
are to do me both a present and a dangerous courtesy.

PROVOST   Pray, sir, in what?

DUKE   In the delaying death.

PROVOST   Alack, how may I do it, having the hour limited and   155
an express command, under penalty, to deliver his head in
the view of Angelo? I may make my case as Claudio's to
cross this in the smallest.

DUKE   By the vow of mine order, I warrant you, if my instructions may be your guide, let this Barnardine be this mor-   160
ning executed, and his head borne to Angelo.

PROVOST   Angelo hath seen them both and will discover the favor.

DUKE   Oh, death's a great disguiser, and you may add to it.
Shave the head and tie the beard, and say it was the desire
of the penitent to be so bared before his death; you know   165
the course is common. If anything fall to you upon this,
more than thanks and good fortune, by the saint whom I
profess, I will plead against it with my life.

PROVOST   Pardon me, good Father, it is against my oath.

DUKE   Were you sworn to the Duke or to the Deputy?   170

PROVOST   To him, and to his substitutes.

DUKE   You will think you have made no offence if the Duke
avouch the justice of your dealing?

PROVOST   But what likelihood is in that?

DUKE   Not a resemblance, but a certainty. Yet since I see you   175
fearful, that neither my coat, integrity, nor persuasion can
with ease attempt you, I will go further than I meant, to
pluck all fears out of you. Look you, sir, here is the hand°
and seal of the Duke; you know the character, I doubt not,
and the signet° is not strange to you?   180

PROVOST   I know them both.

DUKE   The contents of this is the return of the Duke. You shall

made by the Provost; it is as though, having recovered from his initial shock at the enormity of Angelo's duplicity and hypocrisy, the Duke then warms to the idea of punishing him with this elaborate charade and he is pleased by his own inventiveness, even though his plot may seem weak to an audience.

handwriting

official seal

179-93   The Duke is forced to use his own seal (179) to convince the Provost to follow his commands, but he still keeps his actual identity concealed, and he explains that the Duke will return within "two days" (184). The Provost is speechless and clearly shocked by these revelations and plots; his reaction is still one of uncertainty as the Duke reas-

anon over-read it at your pleasure, where you shall find within
these two days he will be here. This is a thing that Angelo
knows not, for he this very day receives letters of strange   185
tenor, perchance of the Duke's death, perchance entering into
some monastery, but by chance nothing of what is writ. Look,
th'unfolding star calls up the shepherd. Put not yourself into
amazement how these things should be; all difficulties are but
easy when they are known. Call your executioner, and off   190
with Barnardine's head. I will give him a present shrift° and advise him for a better place. Yet you are amazed, but this shall
absolutely resolve you. Come away, it is almost clear dawn.

                                                                        [*Exeunt.*]

Scene iii   *Enter* POMPEY.

POMPEY   I am as well acquainted here as I was in our house of
profession. One would think it were Mistress Overdone's own
house, for here be many of her old customers. First, here's
young Master Rash,° he's in for a commodity° of brown paper
and old ginger, nine score and seventeen pounds, of which   5
he made five marks ready money. Marry then, ginger was not
much in request, for the old women° were all dead. Then is
there hereone Master Caper,° at the suit of Master Threepile,°
the mercer,° for some four suits of peach colored satin, which
now peaches° him a beggar. Then have we here young Dizzy,° 10
and young Master Deepvow,° and Master Copperspur,° and
Master Starvelackey,° the rapier and dagger man, and young
Dropheir° that killed lusty Pudding,° and Master Forthright
the tilter,° and brave Master Shoetie° the great traveler, and
wild Halfcan that stabbed Pots, and I think forty more, all   15
great doers in our trade, and are now for the Lord's sake.

                           Enter ABHORSON.

ABHORSON   Sirrah, bring Barnardine hither.

POMPEY   Master Barnadine, you must rise and be hanged,

sures him that all will be well: "Put not yourself into amazement how these things should be" (188). The Provost is still not convinced, a few lines later, as the Duke again tells him "Yet you are amazed". Finally, still being coaxed by the Duke, the two of them leave the stage as dawn arrives, shown on the modern stage by lighting, and perhaps helped with a dawn chorus of birds.

confession

Scene iii

1-15 The morning begins with Pompey alone on stage explaining to the audience how many former customers he recognises in the prison. With grim good-humor he goes through his list of names, all of them containing humorous references to character. This sleepy, slow, early morning mood sets the the tone for the next sequence when Abhorson asks for Bamadine to be brought in. In director Michael Rudman's Caribbean production Pompey "turns his descriptions of his fellow-inmates into an improvised calypso" (*Now*, 15 April 1981).

i.e., Hasty   i.e., badly negotiated loan

i.e., ginger lovers

i.e., Frisky   i.e., Bald

cloth merchant

makes him appear   i.e., Foolish

i.e., Liar in Love   i.e., Worthless

Servant-starver

Heir-killer   i.e., Stuffed-dish

jouster   Shoelace

18-40 Pompey calls out to Bamadine, who is

Master Barnardine.

ABHORSON   What hoa, Barnardine.   20

BARNARDINE   [*Within.*] A pox° o'your throats! Who makes that
noise there? What are you?

POMPEY   Your friends, sir, the hangman. You must be so good,
sir, to rise and be put to death.

BARNARDINE   [*Within.*] Away, you rogue, away, I am sleepy.   25

ABHORSON   Tell him he must awake, and that quickly too.

POMPEY   Pray, Master Barnardine, awake till you are executed
and sleep afterwards.

ABHORSON   Go in to him and fetch him out.

POMPEY   He is coming, sir, he is coming, I hear his straw rustle.   30

Enter BARNARDINE.

ABHORSON   Is the ax upon the block, sirrah?

POMPEY   Very ready, sir.

BARNARDINE   How now, Abhorson? What's the news with you?

ABHORSON   Truly, sir, I would desire you to clap into your
prayers, for look you, the warrant's come.   35

BARNARDINE   You rogue, I have been drinking all night, I am not
fitted for't.

POMPEY   Oh, the better, sir, for he that drinks all night,
and is hanged betimes in the morning, may sleep the sounder
all the next day.   40

Enter DUKE [*disguised as a Friar.*]

ABHORSON   Look you, sir, here comes your ghostly father.° Do
we jest now, think you?

DUKE   [*To* BARNARDINE.] Sir, induced by my charity, and hearing
how hastily you are to depart, I am come to advise you,
comfort you, and pray with you.   45

disease

lying down off stage; from the bad tempered response we learn that he is not pleased to have just been woken up. Pompey, trying to be helpful, suggests to Barnadine, still off stage, that he can sleep again after he has been executed. The black humor continues as Barnadine staggers in, clearly the worse for wear, and declares that in his hung-over state he is not fit to be executed (36) and Pompey continues with his quips.

father confessor

41-58 As the Duke enters (41) Abhorson assumes that with the Friar a more serious tone will ensue, "Do we jest now, think you" (42), but in fact the almost absurd comedy continues as Barnadine refuses to consent to his own execution. The Duke is perplexed by Barnadine's stubborn refusal to cooperate and is caught off guard as Barnadine sweeps off the stage with a regal final announcement (55).

BARNARDINE   Friar, not I, I have been drinking hard all night,
and I will have more time to prepare me, or they shall beat
out my brains with billets.° I will not consent to die this day,
that's certain.

DUKE   Oh, sir, you must, and therefore, I beseech you,   50
Look forward on the journey you shall go.

BARNARDINE   I swear I will not die today for any man's
persuasion.

DUKE   But hear you—

BARNARDINE   Not a word. If you have anything to say to me,   55
come to my ward, for thence will not I today.   *Exit.*

Enter PROVOST.

DUKE   Unfit to live or die. Oh gravel heart!
After him, fellows, bring him to the block.
                                                    [*Exit* ABHORSON *and* POMPEY.]

PROVOST   Now, sir, how do you find the prisoner?

DUKE   A creature unprepared, unmeet for death,   60
And to transport° him in the mind he is
Were damnable.

PROVOST   Here in the prison, Father,
There died this morning of a cruel fever
One Ragozine, a most notorious pirate,
A man of Claudio's years, his beard and head   65
Just of his color. What if we do omit
This reprobate till he were well inclined,
And satisfy the deputy with the visage
Of Ragozine, more like to Claudio?

DUKE   Oh, 'tis an accident that heaven provides.   70
Dispatch it presently, the hour draws on
Prefixed by Angelo. See this be done,
And sent according to command, whiles I
Persuade this rude wretch willingly to die.

PROVOST   This shall be done, good Father, presently.   75
But Barnardine must die this afternoon,

sticks

The two hapless guards, Pompey and Abhorson, clumsily and reluctantly have to chase after him, urged on by the Duke (58).

convey to death

59-93   The Duke, feeling his plans frustrated by Barnadine, complains to the Provost who has just reentered (58). The Provost, however, changes the rhythm of the scene and moves it more rapidly forward away from the ponderous dark humor that has so far dominated. Finishing the Duke's unfinished verse line (62), he offers a quick solution to the dilemma with the idea of using the head of a criminal, Ragozine, who has died of fever this same morning. The Duke builds on this faster-moving, more urgent mood and, reminding us that there is little time left to complete the plan, "the hour draws on" (71), immediately agrees to the proposal.

The Provost, worrying as always about the details and his own security, reminds the Duke that Claudio must not be seen. The Duke, again anxious not to lose time, reassures the Provost of his safety and then commands him quickly to press on with the scheme. Whilst the Provost exits to sever the head of Ragozine (84) the Duke has a brief moment alone on stage, during which he explains to the audience how he will send a message to Angelo announcing his return. During these sequences in particular and throughout Act V, the Duke can either be played as tense and serious in the pursuance of his plot for the sake of justice or as in director Tyrone Guthrie's production, as a man enjoying the emotional chaos around him and revelling in the situation: "the puck-

And how shall we continue Claudio,
To save me from the danger that might come
If he were known alive?

DUKE   Let this be done:
Put them in secret holds, both Barnardine and Claudio;   80
Ere twice the sun hath made his journal greeting
To yond° generation, you shall find
Your safety manifested.

PROVOST   I am your free dependent.

DUKE   Quick, dispatch, and send the head to Angelo.
                                         Exit [PROVOST.]

Now will I write letters to Angelo—   85
The Provost, he shall bear them—whose contents
Shall witness to him I am near at home,
And that by great injunctions I am bound
To enter publicly. Him I'll desire
To meet me at the consecrated fount,°   90
A league below the city, and from thence,
By cold gradation and weal-balanced° form.
We shall proceed with Angelo.

                Enter PROVOST [*with* RAGOZINE'S *head.*]

PROVOST   Here is the head, I'll carry it myself.

DUKE   Convenient is it. Make a swift return,   95
For I would commune with you of such things
That want no ear but yours.

PROVOST   I'll make all speed.   *Exit.*

ISABELLA   [*Within.*] Peace, hoa, be here.

DUKE   The tongue of Isabel. She's come to know
If yet her brother's pardon be come hither,   100
But I will keep her ignorant of her good,
To make her heavenly comforts of despair
When it is least expected.

                        Enter ISABELLA.

ish Duke is skylarking about the dungeon in the garb
of a religious, compounding everybody's agony by
his ideas of a joke…(taking) a Mephistophelean pleasure in drawing out the suspense of Angelo's assort-
ed victims" (*World Journal Tribune*, 15 February
1967).

yonder

fountain

i.e., balanced for the people's
    welfare

94-114   Continuing the rapid forward-moving energy of the scene, the Provost quickly returns with the
severed head in his hand and is immediately dis-
patched to Angelo by the Duke, exiting while finishing another verse line of the Duke's: "I'll make all
speed" (97). As he exits in one direction there is
already the overlapping sound of Isabella arriving
from another (98), thereby continuing the breathless
speed of action on stage.

    In the short moments before she appears,
the Duke again explains to the audience, perhaps
unconvincingly, that he will continue to hold the truth
from Isabella so that the comfort will be greater when
she discovers that her brother is in fact safe. A second, more likely explanation is that the Duke is drawn
to her and wishes to prolong the complex game until
he feels the moment is best for his own purposes. A
third is that he seems to want to observe her reactions, almost as though he is studying her and trying
to weigh her up. In most productions the moment is
often played as a mixture of all three. He watches her

ISABELLA   Hoa, by your leave.

DUKE   Good morning to you, fair and gracious daughter.

ISABELLA   The better given me by so holy a man.   105
   Hath yet the Deputy sent my brother's pardon?

DUKE   He hath released him, Isabel, from the world.
   His head is off, and sent to Angelo.

ISABELLA   Nay, but it is not so.

DUKE   It is no other.
   Show your wisdom, daughter, in your close patience.   110

ISABELLA   Oh, I will to him and pluck out his eyes!

DUKE   You shall not be admitted to his sight.

ISABELLA   Unhappy Claudio, wretched Isabel,
   Injurious world, most damnèd Angelo!

DUKE   This nor hurts him, nor profits you a jot,   115
   Forbear it therefore, give your cause to heaven.
   Mark what I say, which you shall find
   By every syllable a faithful verity.°
   The Duke comes home tomorrow, nay dry your eyes.
   One of our covent,° and his confessor,   120
   Gives me this instance. Already he hath carried
   Notice to Escalus and Angelo,
   Who do prepare to meet him at the gates,
   There to give up their power. If you can pace your wisdom
   In that good path that I would wish it go,   125
   And you shall have your bosom on this wretch,
   Grace of the Duke, revenges to your heart,
   And general honor.

ISABELLA   I am directed by you.

DUKE   This letter then to Friar Peter give,
   'Tis that he sent me of the Duke's return.   130
   Say, by this token, I desire his company
   At Mariana's house tonight. Her cause and yours
   I'll perfect him withal, and he shall bring you
   Before the Duke, and to the head of Angelo
   Accuse him home and home. For my poor self,   135

intently as she responds to his information that Claudio's head has been sent, as requested, to Angelo.

Isabella responds not with sadness but fury: "Oh, I will to him and pluck out his eyes!" (111), as she realizes the extent of Angelo's treachery. The anger gives way to tears of despair as she feels the full weight of the injustice that has been done to her and Claudio (113-114).

truth

religious order

115-40 The Duke tries to persuade Isabella that she can have revenge on Angelo and bring her case to the Duke who is about to return. Lucio's arrival interrupts the proposal and breaks the intimacy between the Duke and Isabella. As he comforts her the Duke is almost whispering his words, probably holding her hands and enjoying the moment of intimacy that is broken by Lucio's arrival. Lucio probably calls out for the Provost before he actually enters (141) thereby causing the Duke to move quickly away from holding Isabella as he asks, with irritation, "Who's here?" (140).

I am combinèd° by a sacred vow
And shall be absent. [*Giving her a letter.*] Wend° you with this
   letter.
Command these fretting waters° from your eyes
With a light heart; trust not my holy order
If I pervert° your course. Who's here?   140

Enter Lucio.

Lucio   Good even. Friar, where's the Provost?

Duke   Not within, sir.

Lucio   Oh pretty Isabella, I am pale at mine heart to see thine
eyes so red. Thou must be patient. I am fain to dine and sup
with water and bran, I dare not for my head fill my belly.   145
One fruitful meal would set me to't, but they say the Duke
will be here tomorrow. By my troth, Isabel, I loved thy brother. If the old fantastical Duke of dark corners had been at
home, he had lived.   [*Exit* Isabella.]

Duke   Sir, the Duke is marvelous little beholding to your   150
reports, but the best is, he lives not in them.

Lucio   Friar, thous knowest not the Duke so well as I do. He's a
better woodman° then thou tak'st him for.

Duke   Well, you'll answer this one day. Fare you well.

Lucio   Nay tarry, I'll go along with thee, I can tell thee pretty   155
tales of the Duke.

Duke   You have told me too many of him already, sir, if they
be true; if not true, none were enough.

Lucio   I was once before him for getting a wench with child.

Duke   Did you such a thing?   160

Lucio   Yes, marry did I, but I was fain to forswear° it, they
would else have married me to the rotten medlar.°

Duke   Sir, your company is fairer than honest. Rest you well.

Lucio   By my troth, I'll go with thee to the lane's end. If bawdy
talk offend you, we'll have very little of it. Nay, Friar, I am   165

bound

go

tears

upset

woman-hunter

143-66   The Duke's irritation increases as he sees that it is Lucio, who has already slandered him earlier in the play (III.i.), particularly as Lucio immediately insults him again, implying that he commits various misdeeds at night: "the old fantastical Duke of dark corners" (148). Isabella, still in distress, exits without further comment (149) and Lucio is left alone with the Duke who abruptly contradicts Lucio's opinions about himself. With a final threat, "Well, you'll answer this one day" (154), the Duke begins to exit. However, in spite of the Duke's ill humor, Lucio is oblivious and decides to accom-pany him whilst offering to tell more ill tales about him. The scene ends on a humorous note as the Duke, by now wishing that he no longer had to maintain his disguise as the Friar and could deal with Lucio, exits with Lucio determined to "stick" (166) at his side. Throughout this scene the actor playing the Duke has to decide how to react to what is happening as events slide out of his control. Lucio causes the audience to laugh at the Duke at the end of the scene, perhaps further damaging his authority and sense of control.

deny

i.e., prostitute

a kind of burr, I shall stick.   *Exeunt.*

Scene iv   *Enter* ANGELO *and* ESCALUS.

ESCALUS   Every letter he hath writ hath disvouched other.

ANGELO   In most uneven and distracted manner, his actions
show much like to madness; pray heaven his wisdom be not
tainted. And why meet him at the gates and reliver° our
authorities there?   5

ESCALUS   I guess not.

ANGELO   And why should we proclaim it in an hour before his
entering, that if any crave redress of injustice, they should
exhibit their petitions in the street?

ESCALUS   He shows his reason for that: to have a dispatch of   10
complaints and to deliver us from devices hereafter, which
shall then have no power to stand against us.

ANGELO   Well, I beseech you, let it be proclaimed betimes i'th
morn. I'll call you at your house; give notice to such men of
sort and suit as are to meet him.   15

ESCALUS   I shall, sir. Fare you well.

ANGELO   Good night.   [*Exit* ESCALUS.]
This deed unshapes me quite, makes me unpregnant
And dull to all proceedings. A deflowered maid,
And by an eminent body that enforced   20
The law against it! But that her tender shame
Will not proclaim against her maiden loss,
How might she tongue° me? Yet reason dares her no,
For my authority bears of a credent bulk
That no particular scandal once can touch   25
But it confounds the breather. He should have lived,
Save that his riotous youth with dangerous sense
Might in the times to come have ta'en revenge
By so receiving a dishonored life

Scene iv

1-17   The Setting has moved back to the palace
as we see Angelo and Escalus discussing the various letters that the Duke has sent. Angelo is clearly
anxious about the situation, in particular the command to hand back power publicly at the city gates
where any citizen can complain of injustice (6-8).
Escalus, in contrast, is pleased at the news of the
Duke's return and seems unconcerned at the unusual commands. As he exits (17) Angelo is left alone to
worry about what he has done to Claudio and
Isabella and whether it could be told to the Duke.
However, the speech does not linger too long on the
threats to himself but is more focused on a growing
feeling of guilt. His conscience is beginning to trouble
him; in spite of his attempt at self-justification that in
the future Claudio might "have ta'en revenge" (28),
he concludes, without pause, on the same verse-line
that ends that justification (30), "Would yet he had
lived". His final rhyming couplet summarizes his
growing sense of having fallen into a world of moral
disarray in which all certitude vanishes (31-32).

surrender

reproach

With ransom of such shame. Would yet he had lived!   30
Alack, when once our grace we have forgot,
Nothing goes right; we would, and we would not.   *Exit.*

Scene v   *Enter* DUKE [*as himself*] *and* FRIAR PETER.

DUKE   These letters at fit time deliver me.
          The Provost knows our purpose and our plot,
          The matter being afoot, keep your instruction
          And hold you ever to our special drift,
          Though sometimes you do blench° from this to that   5
          As cause doth minister. Go call at Flavius's house,
          And tell him where I stay. Give the like notice
          To Valencius, Rowland, and to Crassus,
          And bid them bring the trumpets to the gate.
          But send me Flavius first.

FRIAR PETER   It shall be speeded well.   [*Exit.*]   10

                              Enter VARRIUS

DUKE   I thank thee, Varrius, thou hast made good haste,
          Come, we will walk. There's other of our friends
          Will greet us here anon, my gentle Varrius.   *Exeunt.*

Scene vi   *Enter* ISABELLA *and* MARIANA.

ISABELLA   To speak so indirectly I am loath.
          I would say the truth, but to accuse him so,
          That is your part, yet I am advised to do it,
          He says, to veil full purpose.

flinch

Scene v

1-13   This very short scene is for the Duke to hand the continuation of the plot on to Friar Peter, as the Duke must now only appear to everyone in his real persona. The scene ends with the Duke gathering various important people of Vienna to join him on his reentry to the city. The Roman-sounding names of those friends, perhaps accidentally added from other sources, might well be left out in production! The brevity and poor plotting within this scene and also Scene vi suggest rapid writing, and it is possible to omit them without significant damage to the play in performance.

Scene vi

1-15   Isabella is still confused by the Duke's instructions as she and Mariana prepare for his arrival. However, before they can resolve her questions, Friar Peter enters and draws them away to prepare as the trumpets announce the Duke's arrival.

It is probable that Friar Peter and Friar

MARIANA   Be ruled by him.

ISABELLA   Besides, he tells me that if peradventure   5
    He speak against me on the adverse side,
    I should not think it strange, for 'tis a physic°
    That's bitter to sweet end.

Enter FRIAR PETER.

MARIANA   I would Friar Peter—

ISABELLA   Oh peace, the Friar is come.

FRIAR PETER   Come, I have found you a stand most fit   10
    Where you may have such vantage on the Duke
    He shall not pass you. Twice have the trumpets sounded.
    The generous and gravest citizens
    Have hent° the gates, and very near upon
    The Duke is ent'ring, therefore hence away.   *Exeunt.*   15

Thomas (I.iii) are actually the same character and that the use of a different name is another minor error in the Folio. The reference by Friar Peter to the trumpets, "Twice have the trumpets sounded" (12), suggests a grandeur and ceremonial process.

medicine

reached

ACT V

Scene i   *Enter* Duke, Varrius, Lords, Angelo, Escalus, Lucio,
[Officers] *and* Citizens *at several doors.*

Duke   [*To* Angelo.] My very worthy cousin, fairly met.
    [*To* Escalus.] Our old and faithful friend, we are glad to see
      you.

Angelo and Escalus   Happy return be to your royal grace!

Duke   Many and hearty thankings to you both.
    [*To* Angelo.] We have made inquiry of you, and we hear   5
    Such goodness of your justice that our soul
    Cannot but yield you forth to public thanks
    Forerunning° more requital.

Angelo   You make my bonds still greater.

Duke   Oh, your desert° speaks loud, and I should wrong it
    To lock it in the wards of covert bosom,   10
    When it deserves with characters of brass
    A forted residence 'gainst the tooth of time
    And razure° of oblivion. Give me your hand
    And let the subject see, to make them know
    That outward courtesies would fain proclaim   15
    Favors that keep within. Come, Escalus,
    You must walk by us on our other hand,
    And good supporters are you.

Enter Friar Peter *and* Isabella.

Friar Peter   Now is your time. Speak loud, and kneel before him.

Isabella   Justice, O royal Duke! Vail your regard   20
    Upon a wronged—I would fain have said a maid.°

ACT V. Scene i

1-25   The opening of the Act, formal and ceremonial, with as many attendant citizens as possible
on stage, is designed by the Duke, as part of his
plan, to be as public as possible for the confrontation
with Angelo.

The Duke lulls Angelo into a false sense of
security as he praises him and claims to have had
good reports of his "justice" (6). The Duke stresses to
Angelo the importance of a public show of how
pleased he is with Angelo's rule (14-16). As the Duke
takes the hand of Angelo on one side and Escalus on
the other as though about to process through the city,

anticipating

Friar Peter and Isabella enter (18) as planned. With
prompting from Friar Peter, Isabella throws herself to
the ground at the Duke's feet and cries out for

deserving

"Justice" (20). She begins her speech with this key
word and ends it with a pounding, ringing repetition of
that same word "justice, justice, justice, justice!" (25),
repeating the same earlier reference by the Duke (6).

erasure

maid: i.e., virgin

O worthy Prince, dishonor not your eye
By throwing it on any other object
Till you have heard me, in my true complaint,
And given me justice, justice, justice, justice!   25

DUKE   Relate your wrongs. In what? By whom? Be brief.
Here is Lord Angelo shall give you justice,
Reveal yourself to him.

ISABELLA   O worthy Duke,
You bid me seek redemption of the devil!
Hear me yourself, for that which I must speak   30
Must either punish me, not being believed,
Or wring redress from you. Hear me, oh hear me, here!

ANGELO   My lord, her wits, I fear, are not firm.
She hath been a suitor to me for her brother
Cut off by course of justice.

ISABELLA   By course of justice!   35

ANGELO   And she will speak most bitterly and strange.

ISABELLA   Most strange, but yet most truly will I speak.
That Angelo's forsworn, is it not strange?
That Angelo's a murderer, is't not strange?
That Angelo is an adulterous thief,   40
An hypocrite, a virgin violator,
Is it not strange? And strange?

DUKE   Nay it is ten times strange!

ISABELLA It is not truer he is Angelo
Than this is all as true as it is strange.
Nay, it is ten times true, for truth is truth   45
To th'end of reck'ning.

DUKE   Away with her. Poor soul,
She speaks this in th'infirmity of sense.

ISABELLA   O Prince, I conjure thee, as thou believ'st
There is another comfort than this world,
That thou neglect me not with that opinion   50
That I am touched with madness. Make not impossible
That which but seems unlike. 'Tis not impossible

26-47   Isabella continues her pleading to the Duke, using the same, pounding rhythm that ends her speech with a change from the word "justice" to "hear me, oh hear me, here" (32). Her tone is increasingly dramatic and desperate as she tries to ensure the Duke's attention.

Angelo remains outwardly calm, unmoved and dismissive as he patronizingly suggests to the Duke that she is insane. However, he accidentally uses again the key word "justice" (35) and this provokes Isabella into a bitter, ironical echoing back of his words, thereby interrupting and finishing his verse-line. The pattern repeats as Angelo again tries to lightly dismiss her complaint as bitter and "strange" (36) and Isabella flings back his same word "strange" and builds a rhetorical speech around it. The Duke gently mocks her rhetorical repetition of the word as he tries to end the sequence with his own use of the word "Nay it is ten times strange" (42).

Isabella, completely immersed in her emotions, is oblivious to the Duke's use of humour and continues her theme, this time adding to "strange" the word "truth", that she then also repeats several times. The overall effect is to indeed make her seem obsessive and deranged, in spite of the reality of the situation.

At the end of her speech (45), as is so often the case throughout this rapid and passionate scene, the verse line is finished by another character. It is as though the scene never stops but moves forward as an unstoppable wave of words and emotions. The Duke feigns to believe that she really has lost her senses and asks for her to be taken away. He watches all the time Angelo's reactions and Isabella's as he, the Duke, forces her to respond; he is determined to prolong his game of cat and mouse with the two of them.

48-77   Isabella changes direction and, while maintaining a passionate energy in her speech, she begins to construct a more coherent and subtle argument about the differentiation between what seems to be and what actually is: Angelo has the outward trappings of honor but is in fact an "arch-villain" (57).

The Duke begins to pile the pressure on

But one, the wickedst caitiff on the ground,
May seem as shy, as grave, as just, as absolute
As Angelo. Even so may Angelo,   55
In all his dressings, caracts,° titles, forms,
Be an arch-villain. Believe it, royal Prince!
If he be less, he's nothing, but he's more,
Had I more name for badness.

DUKE   By mine honesty,
If she be mad, as I believe no other,   60
Her madness hath the oddest frame of sense,
Such a dependency° of thing on thing,
As e'er I heard in madness.

ISABELLA   O gracious Duke,
Harp not on that, nor do not banish reason
For inequality, but let your reason serve   65
To make the truth appear where it seems hid
And hide the false seems true.

DUKE   Many that are not mad
Have sure more lack of reason. What would you say?

ISABELLA   I am the sister of one Claudio,
Condemned upon the act of fornication   70
To lose his head, condemned by Angelo.
I, in probation of a sisterhood,
Was sent to by my brother; one Lucio
As then the messenger—

LUCIO   That's I, an't° like your grace.
I came to her from Claudio and desired her   75
To try her gracious fortune with Lord Angelo
For her poor brother's pardon.

ISABELLA   That's he indeed.

DUKE   [*To* LUCIO.] You were not bid to speak.

LUCIO   No, my good lord,
Nor wished to hold my peace.

DUKE   I wish you now then.
Pray you take note of it, and when you have   80
A business for yourself, pray heaven you then

signs

Angelo as he acknowledges a sanity in her words. Realising that the Duke is now listening, she completely changes her approach and suddenly, moving away from the rhetorical phrasing and oblique diction, uses a calmer and simpler manner of speech as she begins to relate the story of what has happened. In this way the mood of the scene abruptly shifts and there is, perhaps, a concentrated silence among all on stage, rather than the whispering and laughter that may have gone before. However, as is so often the case in this ever-changing play, the mood lasts only for a moment before it is broken again, this time by Lucio who opportunistically decides to include himself in the story now that Isabella is being listened to by the Duke (74).

logical dependency

if it

78-87 The Duke, remembering Lucio's past insults, is quick to tell him to be quiet, but there is humour for the audience as Lucio repeatedly tries to involve himself in the unfolding story. Finally, the Duke angrily manages to silence Lucio (87) and Isabella is able to continue.

Be perfect.

LUCIO   I warrant° your honor.

DUKE   The warrant's for yourself; take heed to't.

ISABELLA   This gentleman told somewhat of my tale.

LUCIO   Right.   85

DUKE   It may be right, but you are i'th' wrong
To speak before your time. [*To* ISABELLA.] Proceed.

ISABELLA   I went
To this pernicious caitiff deputy—

DUKE   That's somewhat madly spoken.

ISABELLA   Pardon it,
The phrase is to the matter.   90

DUKE   Mended again. The matter; proceed.

ISABELLA   In brief, to set the needless process by:
How I persuaded, how I prayed and kneeled,
How he refelled° me, and how I replied—
For this was of much length—the vile conclusion   95
I now begin with grief and shame to utter.
He would not but by gift of my chaste body
To his concupiscible intemperate lust
Release my brother; and after much debatement,
My sisterly remorse confutes mine honour,   100
And I did yield to him. But the next morn betimes,
His purpose surfeiting, he sends a warrant
For my poor brother's head.

DUKE   This is most likely.

ISABELLA   Oh that it were as like as it is true!

DUKE   By heaven, fond wretch, you know'st not what thou
        speak'st,   105
Or else thou are suborned° against his honor
In hateful practice. First, his integrity
Stands without blemish; next, it imports no reason
That with such vehemency he should pursue
Faults proper to himself. If he had so offended,   110

assure

refuted

91-126 Isabella briefly tells her tale, pretending, as she was told to by the Duke when he was in disguise (IV.vi.1-4), that she "did yield" (101) to Angelo as he demanded. The plot twists again as the Duke seemingly rejects Isabella's testimony, takes Angelo's part and calls an officer to take her away to prison. The fairly static stage picture breaks as the officer takes her away and the Duke looks around the people on stage to see if anyone will claim to know Friar Lodowick, the name he himself had taken when disguised as a Friar. It is as though, once again, the Duke is testing the integrity of all around him as he suggests that there is a conspiracy connected to that man. He also seems to be enjoying himself as he squeezes every last drop of drama from the scene. Lucio steps forward, seeing another opportunity to ingratiate himself with the Duke.

bribed

He would have weighed thy brother by himself,
And not have cut him off. Someone hath set you on.
Confess the truth, and say by whose advice
Thou cam'st here to complain.

ISABELLA   And is this all?
Then, O you blessèd ministers above,   115
Keep me in patience, and with ripened time
Unfold the evil which is here wrapped up
In countenance. Heaven shield your grace from woe,
As I thus wronged, hence unbelievèd go.

DUKE   I know you'd fain be gone. An officer!   120
To prison with her. [OFFICER *arrests* ISABELLA.] Shall we thus
   permit
A blasting and a scandalous breath to fall
On him so near us? This needs must be a practice.
Who knew of your intent and coming hither?

ISABELLA   One that I would were here, Friar Lodowick.   125
                                        [*Exit with* OFFICER.]

DUKE   A ghostly father, belike. Who knows that Lodowick?

LUCIO   My lord, I know him, 'tis a meddling friar,
I do not like the man. Had he been lay,° my lord,
For certain words he spake against your grace
In your retirement, I had swinged° him soundly.   130

DUKE   Words against me? This a good friar belike,
And to set on this wretched woman here
Against our substitute. Let this friar be found.

LUCIO   But yesternight, my lord, she and that friar,
I saw them at the prison, a saucy° friar,   135
A very scurvy fellow.

FRIAR PETER   Blessèd be your royal grace!
I have stood by, my lord, and I have heard
Your royal ear abused. First hath this woman
Most wrongfully accused your substitute,   140
Who is as free from touch or soil with her
As she from one ungot.°

DUKE   We did believe no less.

non-clerical

beaten

insolent

128-61 Lucio unknowingly insults the Duke yet again, much to the amusement of the audience, as he lies about the Duke's other persona, Friar Lodowick. Friar Peter, however, quickly puts the plot back on course by asking to bring forth Mariana. He lulls Angelo into false security by declaring that this new witness will prove that Angelo did not "touch or soil" (141) Isabella, although in fact the Friar is digging a deeper trap.

Throughout all these last exchanges and those soon to come Angelo has remained silent, trying to show little reaction and appearing bemused, indifferent but never troubled. Lucio, meanwhile, is put out by Friar Peter's defense of Lodowick; he acts hurt that he might be disbelieved and waits for his next moment to strike back.

unbegotten

Know you that Friar Lodowick that she speaks of?

FRIAR PETER   I know him for a man divine and holy,
 Not scurvy, nor a temporary meddler   145
 As he's reported by this gentleman,
 And on my trust, a man that never yet
 Did, as he vouches, misreport your Grace.

LUCIO   My lord, most villanously, believe it.

FRIAR PETER   Well, he in time may come to clear himself,   150
 But at this instant he is sick, my lord,
 Of a strange fever. Upon his mere request,
 Being come to knowledge that there was complaint
 Intended 'gainst Lord Angelo, came I hither
 To speak as from his mouth what he doth know   155
 Is true and false, and what he with his oath
 And all probation will make up full clear
 Whensoever he's convented. First, for this woman,
 To justify this worthy nobleman
 So vulgarly and personally accused,   160
 Her shall you hear disprovèd to her eyes,
 Till she herself confess it.

DUKE   Good Friar, let's hear it.
        [Exit FRIAR PETER.*]*
 Do you not smile at this, Lord Angelo?
 Oh heaven, the vanity of wretched fools!
 Give us some seats. *[Two chairs are brought in.]* Come cousin
  Angelo,   165
 In this I'll be impartial. *[He and* ANGELO *sit.]* Be you judge
 Of your own cause.

    Enter [FRIAR PETER *with*] MARIANA *[Veiled.]*

     Is this the witness, Friar?
 First let her show her face, and after, speak.

MARIANA   Pardon, my lord, I will not show my face
 Until my husband bid me.   170

DUKE   What, are you married?

MARIANA   No, my lord.

162-68 The stage has probably remained relatively informally arranged throughout the first part of the scene. After the processional entrance and Isabella's intervention the Duke has been centrally positioned, with Escalus and Angelo close by, as the other characters, Lucio, and Friar Peter have stepped forward to speak to the Duke, with the other assembled spectators gathered around. Now, there is a deliberate change in pattern indicated as they await the arrival of Mariana. The Duke commands seats to be brought for himself and Angelo so that the arrangement will now look more like a formal court ("Give us some seats" (165)). The Duke deliberately sets Angelo up in the central position so that he is unable to avoid becoming, in effect, the judge of his own case, as the Duke himself states (166). With the other attendant characters circled around the chairs, Angelo is fully focused on, trapped at centre stage as the witness arrives.

The Duke assumes the role of interrogator to Mariana, whilst Angelo must sit closely by and silently watch. Because she is veiled, the drama of the situation is heightened as Angelo anxiously tries to understand what is happening. The Duke clearly enjoys playing out the end-game to his plan that he has consciously made as public as possible to maximize the discomfort and humiliation for Angelo.

169-99 There is silence among the onlookers as the interrogation begins with simple, economical

DUKE   Are you a maid?°

MARIANA   No, my lord.

DUKE   A widow then?   175

MARIANA   Neither, my lord.

DUKE   Why you are nothing then: neither maid, widow, nor wife?

LUCIO   My lord, she may be a punk,° for many of them are
        neither maid, widow, nor wife.

DUKE   Silence that fellow! I would he had some cause to prattle 180
        for himself.

LUCIO   Well, my lord.

MARIANA   My lord, I do confess I ne'er was married,
        And I confess besides I am no maid;
        I have known° my husband, yet my husband   185
        Knows not that ever he knew me.

LUCIO   He was drunk then, my lord, it can be no better.

DUKE   For the benefit of silence, would thou wert so too.

LUCIO   Well, my lord.

DUKE   This is no witness for Lord Angelo.   190

MARIANA   Now I come to't, my lord.
        She that accuses him of fornication,
        In self-same manner doth accuse my husband,
        And charges him, my lord, with such a time
        When I'll depose I had him in mine arms   195
        With all th'effect of love.

ANGELO   Charges she more° than me?

MARIANA   Not that I know.

DUKE   No? You say your husband.

MARIANA   Why just, my lord, and that is Angelo,
        Who thinks he knows that he ne'er knew my body,   200
        But knows, he thinks, that he knows Isabel's.

ANGELO This is a strange abuse! Let's see thy face.

unmarried, i.e., a virgin

prose questions and answers. The tension is broken again by Lucio, unable as always to keep quiet for long, who suggests that she must be a prostitute if, in the Duke's words she is "neither maid, widow, nor wife" (177). The Duke tries to silence Lucio, who is perhaps restrained at this point by a guard, but a few lines later he again tries to puncture the riddles of Mariana's testimony with vulgar humor: "He was drunk then, my Lord" (187). Lucio's unstoppable need to blurt out his opinions is almost like that of a

prostitute

child carried away by the excitement of a game; in this way it amuses the audience as much as it irritates the Duke. Mariana, maintaining her enigmatic version of events implies, ambiguously, that her "husband" is accused of fornication by Isabella. Angelo, confused by the direction that this is all taking, not realizing that he is the "husband" in question, assumes that Isabella has also accused another man. At this moment, probably leaping to his feet, Angelo thinks he has found a way out as this that will discredit what Isabella's claim against him. But, at

sexually known

this same last moment of hope for Angelo, Mariana aims the mortal blow as she identifies Angelo as her "husband" (199).

others

202-22 Mariana theatrically takes off her mask or veil (204) and tells Angelo that it was she that "did

MARIANA   [*Unveiling.*] My husband bids me, now I will unmask.
  This is that face, thou cruel Angelo,
  Which once thou swor'st was worth the looking on.   205
  This is the hand which with a vowed contract
  Was fast belocked in thine. This is the body
  That took away the match from Isabel
  And did supply thee at thy garden-house
  In her imagined person.   210

DUKE   [*To* ANGELO.] Know you this woman?

LUCIO   Carnally, she says!

DUKE   Sirrah, no more!

LUCIO   Enough, my lord.

ANGELO   My lord, I must confess, I know this woman,   215
  And five years since there was some speech of marriage
  Betwixt myself and her, which was broke off,
  Partly for that her promised proportions°
  Came short of composition, but in chief
  For that her reputation was disvalued   220
  In levity.° Since which time of five years
  I never spake with her, saw her, nor heard from her,
  Upon my faith, and honor.

MARIANA   Noble Prince,
  As there comes light from heaven, and words from breath,
  As there is sense in truth, and truth in virtue,   225
  I am affianced this man's wife as strongly
  As words could make up vows. And, my good lord,
  But Tuesday night last gone, in's° garden house,
  He knew me as a wife. As this is true,
  Let me in safety raise me from my knees,   230
  Or else forever be confixèd here
  A marble monument.

ANGELO   I did but smile till now.
  Now, good my lord, give me the scope of justice!
  My patience here is touched; I do perceive
  These poor informal women are no more   235
  But instruments of some more mightier member
  That sets them on. Let me have way, my lord,

supply" (209) him the night before. As the Duke sharply turns to Angelo who is now seated again, he finishes Mariana's verse-line without allowing any pause and asks him, "Know you this woman?" (211). Again, the tension is cracked open by Lucio, who responds before Angelo can, and jokes with the sexual pun on the word "know" (211). The furious Duke silences him and Angelo who, thanks to Lucio, has had a moment to gather his thoughts, tries to discredit her by suggesting that he broke off his relationship with her five years ago because of her tarnished "reputation" (220). From this moment on the actor playing Angelo begins to panic and his silence has to break as he begins to understand that his world of deceit is about to crash open; it is the first time in the scene that we see an expression of emotion from him. Mariana kneels in front of the Duke and reasserts the truth of what she has said.

i.e., dowry

promiscuity

in his

231-257 Suddenly, Angelo leaps back to his feet and seems to explode with anger as he, like Isabella before him, demands "justice" (233). The Duke stands up, agrees to Angelo's request and offers Escalus to take his place in order to assist Angelo in his search for justice. He sends the Provost off to find Lodowick and then exits himself, leaving Escalus and Angelo as judges. This emphatic repetition of a single word is unusual in Shakespeare's plays and in this instance focuses very specifically this central theme of the play.

To find this practice out.

DUKE   Aye, with my heart,
And punish them to your height of pleasure.
Thou, foolish Friar, and thou, pernicious woman,   240
Compact° with her that's gone. Think'st thou thy oaths,
Though they would swear down each particular saint,
Were testimonies against his worth and credit
That's sealed in approbation? You, Lord Escalus,
Sit with my cousin, lend him your kind pains   245
To find out this abuse, whence 'tis derived.
There is another friar that set them on,
Let him be sent for.

FRIAR PETER   Would he were here, my lord, for he indeed
Hath set the women on to this complaint;   250
Your Provost knows the place where he abides,
And he may fetch him.

DUKE   Go, do it instantly.   [*Exit* PROVOST.]
And you, my noble and well-warranted cousin
Whom it concerns to hear this matter forth,
Do with your injuries as seems you best   255
In any chastisement. I for awhile
Will leave you, but stir not you till you have
Well determined upon these slanderers.

ESCALUS   My Lord, we'll do it throughly.°
                              [*Exit* DUKE; ESCALUS *takes his chair*.]
Signior Lucio, did not you say you knew that Friar Lodo-   260
wick to be a dishonest person?

LUCIO   *Cucullus non facit monachum*°: honest in nothing but in his
clothes; and one that hath spoke most villanous speeches of
the Duke.

ESCALUS   We shall entreat you to abide here till he come, and   265
enforce them against him. We shall find this friar a notable°
fellow.

LUCIO   As any in Vienna, on my word.

ESCALUS   Call that same Isabel here once again, I would speak
with her. [*To* ANGELO.] Pray you, my lord, give me leave to   270

conspire

thoroughly

the hood does not make the
monk (Latin)

258-79 As the Duke exits, Escalus sits down and takes over the proceedings by interrogating Lucio who continues with his usual sexual innuendoes and slanders. The Duke, after a very quick change, reenters with the Provost and Isabella.

Lucio increasingly enjoys himself as he warms to his role of witness for the defense and continues to joke as Escalus begins to question Isabella (278). Before she can respond the focus shifts to the disguised Duke, gleefully identified by Lucio: "here comes the rascal I spoke of" (280).

notorious

question, you shall see how I'll handle her.

LUCIO   Not better than he, by her own report.

ESCALUS   Say you?

LUCIO   Marry, sir, I think if you handled her privately, she would
sooner confess; perchance publicly she'll be ashamed.   275

Enter OFFICERS *with* ISABELLA.

ESCALUS   I will go darkly to work with her.

LUCIO   That's the way, for women are light° at midnight!

ESCALUS   Come on, mistress, here's a gentlewoman denies all
that you have said.

Enter DUKE [*disguised as a* FRIAR] *with* PROVOST.

LUCIO   My lord, here comes the rascal I spoke of, here, with   280
the Provost.

ESCALUS   In very good time. Speak not you to him till we call
upon you.

LUCIO   Mum.

ESCALUS   [*To* DUKE.] Come, sir, did you set these women on to   285
slander Lord Angelo? They have confessed you did.

DUKE   'Tis false.

ESCALUS   How? Know you where you are?

DUKE   Respect to your great place, and let the devil
Be sometime honored for his burning throne.   290
Where is the Duke? 'Tis he should hear me speak.

ESCALUS   The Duke's in us, and we will hear you speak.
Look you speak justly.

DUKE   Boldly, at least. But, oh poor souls,
Come you to seek the lamb here of the fox?   295
Good night to your redress! Is the Duke gone?
Then is your cause gone too. The Duke's unjust
Thus to retort your manifest appeal

promiscuous

285-320 The Duke, relishing his final performance as Friar Lodowick, deliberately provokes Escalus by the challenging tone of his responses, and by his attacks on himself as the Duke. Significantly, it is the attacks on the Duke that bring about anger in Escalus for the first time in the play until he shouts out for Friar Lodowick to be taken to prison (320). Now Angelo, feeling back in control of the situation, takes over the interrogation, exactly, perhaps, as the Duke had hoped.

And put your trial in the villain's mouth,
Which here you come to accuse.   300

LUCIO   This is the rascal! This is he I spoke of!

ESCALUS   Why thou unreverend and unhallowed friar!
Is't not enough thou hast suborned these women
To accuse this worthy man, but in foul mouth,
And in the witness of his proper ear,   305
To call him villain, and then to glance from him
To the Duke himself, to tax him with injustice?
Take him hence. To the rack with him! We'll towze° you
Joint by joint, but we will know his purpose.
What? Unjust?

DUKE   Be not so hot! The Duke dare   310
No more stretch this finger of mine than he
Dare rack his own. His subject am I not,
Nor here° provincial. My business in this state
Made me a looker-on here in Vienna,
Where I have seen corruption boil and bubble   315
Till it o'er-run the stew. Laws for all faults,
But faults so countenanced that the strong statutes
Stand like the forfeits in a barber's shop,°
As much in mock as mark.

ESCALUS   Slander to the state!
Away with him to prison!   320

ANGELO   What can you vouch against him, Signior Lucio?
Is this the man that you did tell us of?

LUCIO   'Tis he, my lord. Come hither, goodman bald-pate, do
you know me?

DUKE   I remember you, sir, by the sound of your voice. I met   325
you at the prison, in the absence of the Duke.

LUCIO   Oh, did you so? And do you remember what you said
of the Duke?

DUKE   Most notedly, sir.

LUCIO   Do you so, sir? And was the Duke a fleshmonger°, a   330
fool, and a coward, as you then reported him to be?

pull

of here

i.e., public lists of customer's
    crimes

323-49   Thoroughly delighting in his center-stage
role, Lucio continues to slander Friar Lodowick and
feigns indignation at his responses. There is knowing
laughter for the audience as the Duke protests, "I
love the Duke as I love myself" (337). Escalus is
again incensed by the Friar's words and works himself up into an agitated state as he repeatedly calls
for the Friar and the others to be arrested. As the
Provost attempts to do this a scuffle ensues; Lucio
joins in vociferously to assist the Provost and in the
comic chaos that follows he unmasks the Duke
(349).

fornicator

DUKE   You must, sir, change persons with me ere you make that
        my report. You indeed spoke so of him, and much more,
        much worse.

LUCIO   Oh thou damnable fellow! Did not I pluck thee by the   335
        nose for thy speeches?

DUKE   I protest, I love the Duke as I love myself.

ANGELO   Hark how the villain would close now, after his
        treasonable abuses!

ESCALUS   Such a fellow is not to be talked withal. Away with him   340
        to prison! Where is the Provost? Away with him to prison! Lay
        bolts° enough upon him. Let him speak no more. Away with
        those giglets° too, and with the other confederate companion.

DUKE   Stay, sir, stay a while.   [PROVOST *tries to arrest him.*]

ANGELO   What, resists he? Help him Lucio.   345

LUCIO   Come sir, come sir, come sir. Foh,° sir! Why you
        bald-pated lying rascal! You must be hooded must you?
        Show your knave's visage with a pox to you! Show your
        sheep-biting° face, and be hanged an° hour. Will't not off?
                [*He pulls off the Friar's hood and discovers the* DUKE.]

DUKE   Thou art the first knave that ere mad'st a duke.   350
        First, Provost, let me bail these gentle three.
        [*To* LUCIO.] Sneak not away, sir, for the friar and you
        Must have a word anon. Lay hold on him.
                                          [OFFICER *arrests* LUCIO.]

LUCIO   This may prove worse than hanging.   354

DUKE   [*To* ESCALUS.] What you have spoke, I pardon. Sit you down,
        We'll borrow place of him.   [*He takes* ANGELO'S *chair.*]
                [*To* ANGELO.] Sir, by your leave,
        Hast thou or word, or wit, or impudence
        That yet can do thee office? If thou hast,
        Rely upon it till my tale be heard,
        And hold no longer out.

ANGELO   Oh, my dread° lord,   360
        I should be guiltier than my guiltiness
        To think I can be undiscernible

i.e., chains
lewd girls

Oh!

thieving   in an

350-373 There is once again silence on stage as Escalus and Angelo stand up as they see the Duke. He quips to the stunned Lucio that he has just created a Duke, a task normally taken on by the King. As the Duke turns to tell the Provost to release Friar Peter, Mariana and Isabella, who are by now held by the Provost and guards, Lucio tries to slip off (352); he is stopped by a guard at the Duke's command.

The Duke tells the amazed Escalus to sit and pointedly sits himself in Angelo's vacated chair, thus becoming himself judge again: "We'll borrow place of him" (356). When asked by the Duke to speak, Angelo accepts that the truth is now known and simply completes his role as judge and passes his own death sentence (367). However, the Duke barely listens to Angelo as he finishes his verse-line (368) by calling for Mariana and sending her and Angelo off to be immediately married. At this command Friar Peter, Angelo, Mariana and the Provost leave the stage, leaving the focus on Isabella, Escalus and the Duke.

dreaded

When I perceive your grace, like power divine,
Hath looked upon my passes. Then, good Prince,
No longer session° hold upon my shame,   365
But let my trial be mine own confession.
Immediate sentence then, and sequent death,
Is all the grace I beg.

DUKE   Come hither, Mariana.
[*To* ANGELO.] Say, was't thou ere contracted to this woman?

ANGELO   I was, my lord.   370

DUKE   Go take her hence and marry her instantly.
Do you the office, Friar, which consummate,
Return him here again. Go with him, Provost.
            [*Exeunt* ANGELO, MARIANA, FRIAR PETER, *and* PROVOST.]

ESCALUS   My Lord, I am more amazed at his dishonor
Than at the strangeness of it.

DUKE   Come hither, Isabel.   375
Your friar is now your prince. As I was then
Advertising and holy to your business,
Not changing heart with habit, I am still
Attornied at your service.

ISABELLA   Oh give me pardon
That I, your vassal, have employed and pained   380
Your unknown sovereignty.

DUKE   You are pardoned, Isabel.
And now, dear maid, be you as free to us.
Your brother's death, I know, sits at your heart,
And you may marvel why I obscured myself,
Laboring to save his life, and would not rather   385
Make rash remonstrance° of my hidden power
Than let him so be lost. Oh most kind maid,
It was the swift celerity° of his death,
Which I did think with slower foot came on,
That brained my purpose. But peace be with him,   390
That life is better life, past fearing death,
Than that which lives to fear. Make it your comfort,
So happy is your brother.

public trial

375-403 The mood of the play changes as the Duke plays out the last movement of his plan. If the Duke has for much of the play been played as a ruler often out of control and uncertain of his decisions, this is the moment when he regains a feeling of power and surety of touch. Now that he has revealed his disguise, the practical mechanics of the plan are complete but the spiritual journey has not yet ended. The Duke prolongs the secret of Claudio's reprieve from death until all the central characters have exposed fully their true inner selves. As he confirms to Isabella that her brother is indeed dead she accepts it calmly (393). Throughout this sequence the Duke is watching carefully every response from Isabella as his last, perhaps cruel test of her is played out.

demonstration

speed

ISABELLA   I do, my lord

                    Enter ANGELO, MARIANA, FRIAR PETER *and* PROVOST.

DUKE   For this new-married man approaching here,
            Whose salt° imagination yet hath wronged   395
            Your well defended honor, you must pardon
            For Mariana's sake. But as he adjudged your brother,
            Being criminal, in double violation
            Of sacred chastity and of promise-breach,
            Thereon dependent for your brother's life,   400
            The very mercy of the law cries out
            Most audible, even from his proper tongue,
            `An Angelo for Claudio, death for death.
            Haste still pays haste, and leisure answers leisure;
            Like doth quit like, and measure still for measure°!'   405
            Then, Angelo, thy fault's thus manifested,
            Which though thou would'st deny, denies thee vantage.
            We do condenm thee to the very block
            Where Claudio stooped to death, and with like haste.
            Away with him.

MARIANA   O my most gracious lord,   410
            I hope you will not mock me with a husband?

DUKE   It is your husband mocked you with a husband;
            Consenting to the safeguard of your honor,
            I thought your marriage fit, else imputation,
            For that he knew you might reproach your life   415
            And choke your good to come. For his possessions,
            Although by confutation° they are ours,
            We do enstate and widow you with all
            To buy you a better husband.

MARIANA   O my dear lord,
            I crave no other, nor no better man.   420

DUKE   Never crave him, we are definitive.

MARIANA   [*Kneeling.*] Gentle my liege.

DUKE   You do but lose your labor.
            Away with him to death. [*To* LUCIO.] Now, sir, to you.

lewd

Matthew 7.1-2: "Judge not,
that ye be not judged. For
with what judgement ye
judge, ye shall be judged,
and with what measure ye
mete, it shall be measured
to you again"

403-29   As soon as Angelo, Mariana, Friar Peter
and the Provost reenter, the Duke announces that
Angelo must die in exchange for the death of
Claudio: "death for death" (403) and "measure still for
measure" (405). But, as he commands that Angelo
be taken away to be executed, Mariana intercedes
(410) and begs for him to be spared. When the Duke
refuses mercy, she continues to plead and kneels at
his feet (422); in desperation she turns to Isabella,
perhaps takes hold of her, and pleads with her to
support her request. The Duke, having achieved
exactly the situation that he had ingeniously manipu-
lated, deliberately tightens the screw on Isabella,
testing her to the full as he reminds her that her
brother's death is due to Angelo (429).

disproving

MARIANA   O my good lord! Sweet Isabel, take my part!
 Lend me your knees, and all my life to come   425
 I'll lend you all my life to do you service.

DUKE   Against all sense you do importune her.
 Should she kneel down, in mercy of this fact,
 Her brother's ghost his pavèd° bed would break
 And take her hence in horror.

MARIANA   Isabel,   430
 Sweet Isabel, do yet but kneel by me,
 Hold up your hands, say nothing, I'll speak all.
 They say best men are molded out of faults,
 And for the most, become much more the better
 For being a little bad. So may my husband.   435
 O Isabel, will you not lend a knee?

DUKE   He dies for Claudio's death.

ISABELLA   [*Kneeling.*]   Most bounteous sir,
 Look, if it please you, on this man condemned
 As if my brother lived. I partly think
 A due sincerity governed his deeds   440
 Till he did look on me. Since it is so,
 Let him not die. My brother had but justice,
 In that he did the thing for which he died.
 For Angelo,
 His act did not o'ertake his bad intent,   445
 And must be buried but as an intent
 That perished by the way. Thoughts are no subjects,
 Intents but merely thoughts.

MARIANA   Merely, my lord.

DUKE   Your suit's unprofitable. Stand up I say.
       [ISABELLA *and* MARIANA *rise.*]
 I have bethought me of another fault.   450
 Provost, how came it Claudio was beheaded
 At an unusual hour?

PROVOST   It was commanded so.

DUKE   Had you a special warrant for the deed?

PROVOST   No my good lord, it was by private message.

stone-covered

437-71   Isabella is the first character in the play to rise above personal grievance and desire for revenge as she kneels beside Mariana and adds her voice to Mariana's and begs the Duke to spare Angelo. However, this comes perhaps only after a substantial pause as in the famous Peter Brook production at Stratford-upon-Avon of 1950 where the actress, Barbara Jefford, took an agonizingly long pause before adding her voice to that of Mariana; repeated in director Adrian Noble's production: "when she finally, after an upstage turn and prolonged pause, pleads for Angelo's life..." (*The Guardian*, 18 April 1984). In this way of playing the moment the decision is painful and not easy for Isabella. However, it is also possible to show Isabella as already sympathetic to Mariana and quick to show emotional female solidarity and perhaps Isabella can embrace her before pleading on her behalf. The short verse line (444) suggests that even having declared her support for mercy, she still swallows and finds it difficult to talk about Angelo and what he has done. Finally, though, she surprises everyone by finding compassion for Angelo and even by trying to understand what he has done as she declares that it was meeting her that corrupted him away from honest intentions (441-442). The Duke can hardly hide his pleasure at her extraordinary gesture of forgiveness as he plays out the final moments of his elaborate game and prompts the Provost to declare that one prisoner, Barnadine, has been spared.

Angelo, either showing genuine repen-

DUKE   For which I do discharge you of your office.   455
   Give up your keys.

PROVOST   Pardon me, noble lord,
   I thought it was a fault, but knew it not,
   Yet did repent me after more advice.
   For testimony whereof, one in the prison
   That should by private order else have died,   460
   I have reserved alive.

DUKE   What's he?

PROVOST   His name is Barnardine.

DUKE   I would thou hadst done so by Claudio.
   Go fetch him hither, let me look upon him.   [*Exit* PROVOST.]

ESCALUS   I am sorry one so learned and so wise
   As you, Lord Angelo, have still appeared,   465
   Should slip so grossly, both in the heat of blood°
   And lack of tempered judgement afterward.

ANGELO I am sorry that such sorrow I procure,
   And so deep sticks it in my penitent heart,
   That I crave death more willingly than mercy,   470
   'Tis my deserving, and I do entreat it.

         Enter PROVOST, BARNARDINE, CLAUDIO [*hooded*] *and* JULIET,
                        [*with a baby.*]

DUKE   Which is that Barnadine?

PROVOST   This, my lord.

DUKE   There was a friar told me of this man.
   Sirrah, thou art said to have a stubborn soul
   That apprehends no further than this world,   475
   And squar'st thy life according. Thou'rt condemned,
   But for those earthly faults, I quit them all,
   And pray thee take this mercy to provide
   For better times to come. Friar, advise him,
   I leave him to your hand. What muffled fellow's that?   480

PROVOST   This is another prisoner that I saved,
   Who should have died when Claudio lost his head,

tance and acknowledgment of grief or desperately trying to show such emotions, reaffirms the judgment that he does deserve to be spared. There is little said and minimum textual evidence for deciding how genuine or not his sudden sense of regret really is; many productions have differed in their final interpretation of Angelo's last moments in the play.

passion

471-97 The theatricality of this play continues through to the end as the Provost, Barnadine and Juliet enter, accompanied by the hooded figure of Claudio (471). As the Duke pretends not to know who is under the hood, the Provost reveals him to be Claudio. As the onlookers gasp, Angelo begins to break down with emotion for the first time in the play and Claudio looks at Isabella in silence, the Duke takes Isabella's hand and proposes marriage. As the Duke stands by her side, Claudio holds Juliet and Angelo stands by his new wife Mariana in apparent reconciliation. Lucio tries to slip off until stopped by the Duke (494).

As like almost to Claudio as himself.

               [PROVOST *removes* CLAUDIO'S *hood*.]

DUKE   [*To* ISABELLA.] If he be like your brother, for his sake
      Is he pardoned, and for your lovely sake   485
      Give me your hand and say you will be mine,
      He is my brother too. But fitter time for that.
      By this Lord Angelo perceives he's safe;
      Methinks I see a quick'ning° in his eye.
      Well, Angelo, your evil quits you well.   490
      Look that you love your wife; her worth, worth yours.
      I find an apt remission in myself,
      And yet here's one in place I cannot pardon.
      [*To* LUCIO.] You, sirrah, that knew me for a fool, a coward,
      One all of luxury, an ass, a madman.   495
      Wherein have I so deserved of you
      That you extol me thus?

LUCIO   'Faith, my lord, I spoke it but according to the trick. If
      you will hang me for it you may, but I had rather it would
      please you I might be whipped.   500

DUKE   Whipped first, sir, and hanged after.
      Proclaim it, Provost, round about the city,
      If any woman wronged by this lewd fellow,
      As I have heard him swear himself there's one
      Whom he begot with child, let her appear,   505
      And he shall marry her. The nuptial finished,
      Let him be whipped and hanged.

LUCIO   I beseech your highness, do not marry me to a whore!
      Your highness said even now I made you a Duke; good my
      lord, do not recompence me in making me a cuckold.°   510

DUKE   Upon mine honor, thou shalt marry her.
      Thy slanders I forgive, and therewithal
      Remit° thy other forfeits.° Take him to prison,
      And see our pleasure herein executed.

LUCIO   Marrying a punk, my lord, is pressing to death,   515
      Whipping and hanging!

DUKE   Slandering a prince deserves it.

               [OFFICERS *exeunt with* LUCIO.]

restoration of life

498-517 In the humorous exchanges that follow, much to the amusement to all on stage, the Duke promises to marry Lucio to the prostitute that he earlier boasted to have made pregnant and deserted; for Lucio this is the worst imaginable fate. However, in the end in spite of all his slanders and misdeeds, it is his quick wit that saves him.

husband of an adulterous wife

cancel   punishments

She, Claudio, that you wronged, look you restore.
Joy to you, Mariana. Love her, Angelo;
I have confessed her, and I know her virtue.   520
Thanks, good friend Escalus, for thy much goodness,
There's more behind that is more gratulate.°
Thanks, Provost, for thy care and secrecy,
We shall employ thee in a worthier place.
Forgive him, Angelo, that brought you home   525
The head of Ragozine for Claudio's,
Th'offense pardons itself. Dear Isabel,
I have a motion° much imports your good,
Whereto if you'll a willing ear incline,
What's mine is yours, and what is yours is mine.   530
So bring us to our palace, where we'll show
What's yet behind that's meet you all should know.

                                           [*Exeunt Omnes.*]

518-32   In the final speech of the play the mood is one of apparent harmony and reconciliation; many of the characters have completed a long spiritual journey and have learnt much about themselves. Although the Duke strikes a happy note of celebration, many questions are left unanswered as we wonder about the likely relationship between Mariana and Angelo and how Isabella feels about becoming the bride of the Duke instead of that of Christ. In some productions Isabella embraces him and clearly accepts, but in others this is not so. In Barry Kyle's 1978 Royal Shakespeare Company' production, the two left the stage closely side by side and overtly happy; in John Barton's 1970 Royal Shakespeare Company production, the audience were left not knowing her final response as she stood speechless, shocked by the suddenness of the proposal; in Nicholas Hytner's 1987 Royal Shakespeare Company version Isabella turned her back on the Duke as though thinking about the future whilst lost in her own world; in Trevor Nunn's 1991 Royal Shakespeare Company staging at the Other Place theatre in Stratford-upon-Avon, the Freudian journey depicted throughout the production came to a natural, sexual end as the Duke and Isabella seemed to accept the physical and spiritual attraction that had been building all the time.

congratulatory

proposal

Textual Notes

Although a performance of *Measure for Measure* was recorded as early as December 26, 1604, the earliest surviving printed text of the play dates from 1623, in the first printed collected edition of Shakespeare's plays known as the First Folio. Because of the dramatic unevenness and inconsistencies in this Folio text, the type and characteristics of the manuscript (which does not survive) from which it was printed have been the subject of much editorial controversy and speculation. Most modern editors agree that the Folio text was printed from a transcript of Shakespeare's original complete draft or "foul papers" rather than of the finalized, master-copy or "prompt-book" used in the theater by the King's Men, Shakespeare's acting company. This transcript was apparently copied by Ralph Crane, a professional scribe who prepared the manuscripts used to print several other Shakespearian plays in the Folio. The Folio text of *Measure for Measure* preserves at least three stages of the play's transmission: its original composition by 1604 (and possible later revision) by Shakespeare; its transcription by Crane by 1622, possibly incorporating theatrical practices after 1604; and its preparation to serve as printer's copy for the First Folio.

The uniquely Shakespearian characteristics that mark the Folio text as deriving from the author's original composition and "foul papers" include the use of: generic speech-prefixes for characters, even though they have character names (for example, Mistress Overdone is termed "Bawd" and Pompey "Clown" in the speech-prefixes but are called by name in the dialogue); minimal (rather than explicit and theatrical) stage directions which are sometimes inconsistent, especially in lacking exit directions for characters who, according to the dialogue, clearly leave the stage and re-enter later; "duplications" in speech or action (sometimes called "repetition-brackets"), as in I.ii, in which Mistress Overdone announces to Lucio and his friends that Claudio has been arrested and then appears surprised a few lines later when Pompey tells her of Claudio's arrest; and "false starts" such as "ghost" or near-ghost characters that Shakespeare included early in a stage direction but for whom he provides little or no dialogue, as well as other confusions in character, plot, structure, and time-scheme. For example, some of the Duke's speeches, particularly in the opening speech in I.i and in IV.i during

Isabella and Mariana's private discussion, appear to have been cut or left incomplete and are thus difficult to understand.

However, in the particular case of *Measure for Measure*, scholars and editors have been far too determined to assign these "errors" to someone other than Shakespeare in order to absolve him of seeming careless or sloppy or indeed anything less than an author who produced flawless texts during composition. The Folio text's inconsistencies actually demonstrate that Shakespeare was already reworking this complexly plotted and structured play while still in the act of composing it. He made numerous revisions in character, plot, dialogue, and structure (during this time period, authors often made revisions in the margin of a manuscript or on inserted slips of paper, and these revisions could be easily overlooked or misconstrued by the next person, whether scribe or compositor, who handled the foul papers). Many scholars have criticized the supposed duplication in I.ii and have debated whether the first announcement (by Mistress Overdone) or the second (by Pompey) of Claudio's arrest was the first that Shakespeare wrote, basing their conclusion on which passage is "more Shakespearian," that is, which is "better." Shakespeare may have rewritten the scene during composition, intending to cancel one of the two discussions and did not do so, or he may not have noticed that he had produced this duplication (other uncorrected duplications appear in *Julius Caesar* and *Love's Labor's Lost*). However, the duplication may have been intentional, for Pompey does not name Claudio as the "yonder" man who has been arrested, and Mistress Overdone's questioning of Pompey introduces dialogue that builds on her earlier statements to Lucio on the consequences of the anti-fornication laws on the profession of bawd. In performance, this "duplication" and other Folio text inconsistencies are not easily recognizable to a theatrical audience and only become problematic to editors eager to present a flawless text to a literary audience.

Although Ralph Crane did not correct these particularly Shakespearian authorial characteristics when he copied Shakespeare's foul papers into the transcript used for the Folio printer's copy, he apparently altered the play in the same way that he altered his transcripts of other plays of the period. He probably supplied the cast-list printed at the end of the Folio text, which names the Duke "Vincentio," and added the formal act-scene divisions. He also hyphenated compound words, routinely inserted apostrophes, colons, and parentheses, regularized speech-prefixes and act-scene divisions, made elisions, and repeated unusal spellings. In other words, Crane made significant grammatical corrections, but he did not change or correct dialogue, theme, character, or structure, except possibly in editing out profanity. The Folio text has been purged of "oaths" (swear words), especially "God," probably as a result of the 1606 act against profanity on the stage; if Crane did not purge the text, he may have been copying from an earlier manuscript that had already cut the oaths. What does seem clear is that Crane was not copying from the King's Men's "book" or theatrical prompt-book used in the theatre to prompt actors during performance. A prompt-book copyist would have indeed corrected the theatrical inconsistencies, such as the missing exit directions, which would have disturbed performance and which still remain in the text.

Thus the Folio text displays a layer of authorial composition and revision, a layer of scribal correction and possibly some minor theatrical alteration, such as the elimination of oaths, and a layer of minor alteration that was inevitable when the compositors set the type in 1622. For example, such errors as "tonch'd" (for "touch'd") in I.ii and "teemiug" (for "teeming") in I.iv are clearly compositorial, resulting from a letter printed upside down. The Folio compositors appeared to have introduced only minor alterations into the text and cannot be credited with the striking inconsistences for which Shakespeare and/or Crane must be held responsible. Yet some editors have continued to argue that the text is so uneven and inconsistent because it was adapted by another author, possibly Thomas Middleton, after Shakespeare's death in 1616 but before its transcription by Crane for the 1623 Folio. These editors cite at least four examples of non-authorial adaptation in the text, including: the appearance in IV.i of the first stanza of a song which later appears (with a second stanza) in a late 1610's King's Men's play, *Rollo, Duke of Normandy, Or, The Bloody Brother*; the possibile transposition of two of the Duke's soliloquies in III.i ("He who the sword of heaven will bear...And perform an old contracting") and IV.i ("O place and greatness, millions of false eyes...And rack thee in their fancies"); the possible addition of I.ii from the beginning of the scene to the entrance of Pompey; the possible alteration of a stage direction in I.iii (I.ii in this text) and elsewhere, and the following dialogue to make Juliet less of a "ghost" character.

However, no conclusive evidence exists to prove that Middleton or any other dramatist altered or adapted the play before 1623, and other explanations can be used to nullify such arguments. For example, the presence of the

IV.i song in both *Measure for Measure* and the later play, *Rollo, Duke of Normandy* (which adds a second stanza) suggests only that the King's Men recycled songs whenever possible, as in the case of Macbeth, whose Folio text includes cues, but not the verses, for two songs which appear in Middleton's *The Witch* In addition, the scene in which the song appears in *Rollo* was apparently written by John Fletcher, so the theory that Middleton and another dramatist such as John Webster would have added a song by Fletcher to *Measure for Measure* when they were serving as the play's adapters is difficult to support. Also, many of the Duke's speeches, beginning with his first in the play's opening lines, seem dramatically and linguistically alienated from their context, suggesting that Shakespeare was presenting a man alienated from his own environment. If his speeches in III.i and IV.i are seen in the same way, there is no reason to suppose they originally belonged elsewhere but were later transposed by an adapter. Lastly, the nine-months pregnant Juliet is not a "ghost" character in I.ii and V.i whom Shakespeare added to the stage directions but forgot to portray in action or dialogue. Instead, she appears as a visual symbol of the natural consequences of sexual intercourse that Angelo cannot succeed in prohibiting, and thus she need not speak in each scene in which she appears. However, the play was adapted after its printing in 1623, first by William Davenant in 1662 and then by Charles Gildon, whose version was printed in 1700.

The printed text of *Measure for Measure* represents the collaborative process through which a play-text passed during its transmission from the author to the actors to the theatrical audience to the copyist to the printers to the reading audience. Most importantly, the text's inconsistencies show us a dramatist at work, writing and rewriting his text, a pattern Shakespeare, as a revising author, used in many of his other plays. The present edition is based on the First Folio, but some stage directions have been expanded or added and are printed in square brackets. Spelling and punctuation have been modernized. Some lines incorrectly printed as verse have been changed to prose, and some verse lines have been relineated, especially when the compositors seem to have run out of room in the right margin and incorrectly printed one verse line as two lines. One major change in scene-numbering has been made: the Folio's scene-division for I.iii at the entrance of Claudio, the Provost and others has been deleted, placing this scene still within I.ii (with the following scenes in Act I renumbered). Although some editors divide Act III into two scenes after Isabella's first exit, this edition retains the

Folio's designation of Act III as one continuous scene. The following collation lists substantive changes from the text of the Folio; the reading of this
edition is quoted first in italics, followed by the rejected Folio reading,
which is printed in Roman type.

I.i.   35 *touched* tonch'd
I.iii 5 *sisterhood* sisterstood   44 *teeming* teemiug

II.i.   38 *Some...fall* Some...fall [printed in italics in F]
II.iv. 24 *swoons* Swounds   75 *craftily* crafty   76 *Let me be* Let
        be   94 *all-binding* all-building   158 *report* reporr 185 *More*
        "More

III.i. 31 *serpigo* sapego   40 *more* moe   90 *enew* emmew.
        392 *dearer* deare

IV.i.   59 *quests* Quest
IV.ii. 96 *This is his lord's man* DUKE This is his lord's man
        97 *DUKE And here comes Claudio's pardon* PROVOST
        And here comes Claudio's pardon   165 *bared* bar'de
IV.iii. 13 *Forthright* Forthlight   15 *Pots* pots
IV.iv. 5 *our authorities* ou rauthorities

V.i.   13 *me* we   197 *more* moe

Grace Ioppolo

Editor: *Measure For Measure*

Grace Ioppolo is a Lecturer in English at the University of Reading, England. She is the author of *Revising Shakespeare* and the editor of *Shakespeare Performed: Essays in Honor of R.A. Foakes*. She has also published numerous essays on English Renaissance Drama.

Leon Rubin

Commentary: *Measure For Measure*

Leon Rubin is Professor of Drama and Theatre Arts at Middlesex University, England. He is also Head of the Asian Performance Research Centre there and the acclaimed International MA/MFA in Theatre Directing. He is a well known theatre director and trainer of actors in numerous countries of the world, on Broadway and London's West end and is former Artistic Director of the major UK theatres: Lyric Theatre, Belfast, Watford Palace Theatre and the Bristol Old Vic. He is also the first foreigner to have been made an Honorary professor of the Russian Academy of Theatre in Moscow (GITIS). He also conducts masterclasses and workshops on acting and directing Shakespeare across the globe. In addition to many papers he has also published the section on S.E. Asian Theatre in the *Oxford Illustrated History of Theatre* and his book *The Nicholas Nickleby Story*, about the making of the historic Royal Shakespeare Company production, for which he was also Assistant Director. He is also a consultant and advisor on all aspects of theatre to various governments and arts organizations in many countries.